fareWel

fareWel

BY IAN ROSS

fareWel
first published 1997 by
Scirocco Drama
An imprint of J. Gordon Shillingford Publishing Inc.
© 1996 Ian Ross

Cover design by Terry Gallagher/Doowah Design
Author photo by Debra Mosher
Scirocco Drama Editor: Dave Carley
Printed and bound in Canada

We acknowledge the support of The Canada Council for the Arts
for our publishing program.

Canadian Cataloguing in Publication Data

Ross, Ian, 1968-
farewel

ISBN 1-896239-21-8

I. Title.

PS8585.O84014F37 1997   C812'.54   C97-900240-0
PR9199.3.R598F37 1997

Acknowledgements

God. My father and mother. Robert Noble. Chris Johnson. Michael Springate. Kim McCaw. Allen MacInnis. My granny and grampa. All of my family (including aunts, uncles, cousins and siblings). The Black Hole Theatre Group. Debra Mosher. Frank Ross. Jean Courchene. Ardis Courchene. Erin Murdoch. Sherri Gould. Andrew Anderson. Archie Woodhouse. Gordon Letandre. The Banff Centre for the Arts. Eadie Russell. Everyone involved in the Banff Playwrights' Colony 1994. Drew Hayden Taylor. Iris Turcott. David Ross. Urjo Kareda. Candace Burley. Bob Baker. All the actors who've worked on the script. Dave Carley. Gordon Shillingford. Winnipeg's artistic community. Wanda Wuttunee. Libby Mason. Marina Endicott. Sarah Endicott. Gylian Raby. Bob Allen. Linda Huffman. The Manitoba Arts Council. John Kim Bell. The Canadian Native Arts Foundation. Cairn Moore and PTE's Adult Company. Prairie Theatre Exchange. Everyone who works at PTE. Cherry Karpyshin. Liana Sanders. Christine Devenney. Lester Ross. Renata Meconse. Greg Ross. Melinda Tallin. Carol Shields. George Amabile. Kim Selody. Leslee Silverman. Monica Marx. Harry Rintoul. Rory Runnells. The Manitoba Association of Playwrights. Bruce McManus. Vic Cowie. All my teachers, friends and anyone I may have forgotten.

Production Credits

fareWel premiered on March 7, 1996, at Prairie Theatre Exchange, Winnipeg, Canada, with the following cast:

MELVIN .... Ryan Black
NIGGER .... Lorne Cardinal
ROBERT .... Mark Dieter
PHYLLIS .... Marsha Knight
TEDDY .... Michael Lawrenchuk
RACHEL .... Tracey McCorrister

Directed by Libby Mason
Set and costume design by Kim Hamin
Lighting design by Bill Williams
Original music score by Greg Lowe
Assistant Director: Monica Marx
Assistant set and costume designer: Louis Ogemah
Stage Manager: Rose Passante
Assistant Stage Manager: Wayne Buss!

Characters

MELVIN McKay: Young and intelligent. Sniffs gas.

Sheldon Traverse (NIGGER): Difficult to discern his age, anywhere from 40-70. Lived a hard life, but survives.

RACHEL Traverse: Sheldon's cousin. 25-35 years old. Strong and beautiful. Wise from life, but hardened by it as well.

PHYLLIS Bruce: Rachel's best friend. 30-40 years old. A little overweight. She possesses a warm and caring spirit.

TEDDY Sinclair: Runs a small pawn shop on the Reserve. A clever man with only one true friend, Sheldon.

ROBERT Traverse: Rachel's cousin. Runs a plumbing and septic service on the Reserve. Wealthy by Reserve standards, middle-class by other standards.

Setting

The Partridge Crop Reserve somewhere in Manitoba's Interlake.

Time

The present.

Playwright's Note

My mother was an invaluable aid in helping with the Saulteaux in *fareWel*. The dialect is Manitoban. Spelling is "as it sounds" rather than as it possibly should be. I've also done the same with many of the English words in *fareWel*, writing them as I hear the characters speak them.

A brief glossary of Saulteaux words used in the text:

Ahneen	(Greeting) How are you?
Meegwetch	Thank you
Boo-zhoo	Hello
Aow i tha	"That's it for now."
Mahjan	Go
Pisahnabin	Shutup
Aweenuk	An insult to a man
Akitten	An insult to a woman
Animush	Dog
Ahnamay igamik	Church

Ian Ross

Ian Ross was born in McCreary, Manitoba, and spent the first five years of his life in the Métis community of Kinosota before moving to Winnipeg, where he has resided ever since. He has been writing plays for five years, and *fareWel* marks his first professional mainstage production. Ian has been a mainstay at the Winnipeg Fringe Festival since 1991, having written *Don't Eat Any Red Snow*, *CDED*, *King of Saturday Night*, *Zombies*, and *Residue of Pain*.

ACT I

(*The play opens in darkness. As the lights come up, the sound of a drum, beating slowly, accompanied by a faint song, is heard. Light begins to seep through the cracks in the doors of a church, warming the area where MELVIN sits. The church is identified by a sign proclaiming "The Partridge Crop Pentecostal Church". Music coming from inside the church increases in volume as the lights come up. It is "Are You Washed in the Blood?" and it has a distinct country feel. The music from the church overpowers the drum, which slowly fades. MELVIN looks a lot younger than he is. He's dressed in dirty jeans, runners, a red shirt and a baseball team jacket with the logo "A's". The back reads "Partridge Crop A's". The number 8 is on his sleeve. MELVIN gets up and paces a bit, uncertain and restless for no apparent reason. Children can be heard running around, laughing.*)

MELVIN: You kids go home. Go home I said.

(*More laughter is heard.*)

I'm gonna tell your mom. You're not supposed to play around the church. Go home.

(*The sound of the children fades slightly. MELVIN sits down on the steps. The door opens, increasing the volume of "Are You Washed in the Blood?" as well as the light. Sheldon (NIGGER) Traverse exits. He's finishing off one salmon sandwich and has another in his hand. NIGGER's body is full of scars which are mostly hidden by clothes. He's dressed in very dirty jeans, very old oxfords and an old sweater. He's wearing a farmer's cap which has a logo of a*)

*beaten-up Native hockey player and the words,
"Dakota Ojibway Teepee Creepers". NIGGER's
face is rough and his complexion dark, very dark.)*

You kids get home I said. *(MELVIN notices
NIGGER.)* Those stupid kids. That Phyllis has to
learn to look after them better. They shouldn't be
playing around here. The chief should make it so no
kids can play around the church.

NIGGER: Maybe when he gets back from Vegas.

*(NIGGER pulls a half-smoked cigarette out of his
pocket.)*

Got a light?

MELVIN: No.

NIGGER: Oh. *(He proceeds to eat his sandwich and look for a light
on his person. Eventually, he sits beside MELVIN and
takes off one of his shoes, removes some matches and
lights his smoke. He alternates smoking and biting his
sandwich.)* Boy, you want some of this? I never had
one of these fish samiches before. They're really
good.

MELVIN: Don't do that.

NIGGER: What?

MELVIN: Smoke.

NIGGER: Aaaaannnnnhhh.

MELVIN: Don't smoke and eat.

NIGGER: You're not eating. I like a smoke with a meal.

MELVIN: After. After a meal. Not while you're eating.

NIGGER: What the hell's the matter with you anyways?

MELVIN: This is a church. If you want to smoke go on the
road.

NIGGER: You go smoke on the road.

MELVIN:	I don't smoke. This is church. You don't smoke here.
NIGGER:	I'll smoke wherever the hell I want.
MELVIN:	You're as bad as those kids. This is holy ground. You have to respect this place.
NIGGER:	Oh. You want some of this samich? I never had pink fish before.
MELVIN:	That's salmon.
NIGGER:	Yeah? You think it's from B.C.?
MELVIN:	Prob'ly.
NIGGER:	That's one good thing about wakes.
MELVIN:	What's that?
NIGGER:	The food. I wasn't even gonna come tonight. I'm glad old Angus died.

(MELVIN punches NIGGER in the arm. Hard.)

MELVIN:	Watch what you say?
NIGGER:	What?
MELVIN:	A wake is for grieving. Not eating.
NIGGER:	Then why do they have food in there then?
MELVIN:	Because you're supposed to sing and pray all night. Some of these people won't go home until tomorrow.
NIGGER:	Aaahh. What the hell's the matter with you anyways?
MELVIN:	I just don't like people disrespecting this place.
NIGGER:	Well go in there and get some food. Or pray or sing or something. *(He gets up and raises his hands in the air.)* Praise Jesus.
MELVIN:	Praise Jesus.

(NIGGER finishes off the sandwich and contorts his face.)

NIGGER: Hmm. Is there s'posed to be bones in salmon?

MELVIN: Of course.

NIGGER: I think I just bit one.

(NIGGER rubs his cheek. The sound of the children's laughing increases. NIGGER notices them.)

You kids put that dog down. Hey. *(NIGGER starts laughing.)*

MELVIN: That dog's gonna bite you.

NIGGER: Hey. *(NIGGER runs off.)*

MELVIN: Just let them get bit.

(We hear NIGGER calling out. The sound of the children laughing fades under that of a dog barking.)

(Lights up on RACHEL sitting at the table in PHYLLIS' house, running her hand along part of a dancing outfit. RACHEL has long, dark hair and is dressed in a blouse and ripped jeans (not to be stylish, but because they're her only pair). PHYLLIS' house is rather messy, and there is evidence everywhere of children. There is a dull thump against the door. RACHEL ignores it.)

PHYLLIS: *(Off.)* Do you want some tea?

RACHEL: What?

PHYLLIS: I said, do you want some tea?

RACHEL: Yeah. *(RACHEL puts the outfit down and picks through the butts in the ashtray.)*

(The dull thump continues. PHYLLIS comes from offstage and throws open the door. PHYLLIS is a larger woman with a strong body. She is wearing slacks and a T-shirt. She screams.)

PHYLLIS: You kids stop throwing that ball against the house.

Go play at the dump. *(She shuts the door.)* Damn kids. Did you say you wanted tea? *(She exits to the kitchen.)*

RACHEL: Yeah. D'you have any smokes?

PHYLLIS: Yeah. In my jacket.

(RACHEL looks in PHYLLIS' jacket. She searches all the pockets, pulling out more and more crap. Tissues, candy bar wrappers, matches, and finally an empty pack of cigarettes. RACHEL, dejected, slumps slightly.

(Off.) You should have seen that stupid Nigger at the wake. He was there pretending to try and sing, "Jesus in the Family", but he kept saying it "pamily", like if you're from Dauphin River. And you could just hear him. *(PHYLLIS comes in, singing.)* "Jesus in the pamily, happy happy home."

RACHEL: You don't got any.

PHYLLIS: What?

RACHEL: Cigrettes.

PHYLLIS: *(She sits with the tea.)* Those damn kids. That Jamie's stealing my cigrettes again. He's just like his dad that one, never listening to me. *(She notices the dancing outfit.)* See. Look at this I told him to throw this stupid old thing out.

RACHEL: No. Don't. I took that out of the garbage. You shouldn't throw this out Phyllis.

PHYLLIS: Yes. It's heathen this thing. I just didn't want to say no when Bertha gave it to me.

RACHEL: You disrespect Angus by throwing this out you know?

PHYLLIS: I don't want it.

RACHEL: Well I'll keep it then.

PHYLLIS: If you cared so much about Angus how come you didn't stay at the wake?

RACHEL:	I feel bad enough already.
PHYLLIS:	About what?
RACHEL:	There's never anything good around this place. You notice that? There's always people dying, or waiting to die. I should've just stayed in Winnipeg.
PHYLLIS:	Then who would I talk to?

(RACHEL sips her tea.)

RACHEL:	This tea tastes funny.
PHYLLIS:	I don't got any new bags.
RACHEL:	Well could you get me some sugar.
PHYLLIS:	I don't got none left. I'm trying to cut back.
RACHEL:	Why?
PHYLLIS:	The nurse at school's been scaring the shit out of me and my kids. She told them they're gonna get sugar di-betes, 'cause that's what happens to Indian kids who eat too much sugar.
RACHEL:	Ahhh those doctors and nurses are full of shit. They don't care about us. They come here, feel our heart, pull our teeth and then take off and get their money from the government. They don't give a shit about us.

(RACHEL begins picking up different butts and looking at them.)

PHYLLIS:	I'll help you. You think we'll have enough for two?
RACHEL:	Don't know. Probably.

(They begin to take what tobacco they can out of the remaining butts.)

PHYLLIS:	You know Rachel…
RACHEL:	Yeah?
PHYLLIS:	I'm kinda scared.

(There's a loud thump at the door. PHYLLIS jumps. She gets up and throws the door open. She yells.)

You kids stop that. Go play at the dump I said. And Jamie you stop stealing my cigrettes, you'll get addicted. Damn kids.

RACHEL: They're just playing.

PHYLLIS: They don't have to use the side of the house like a barn. *(PHYLLIS sits back down.)*

RACHEL: What?

PHYLLIS: Eh?

RACHEL: Forget it. What were you saying?

PHYLLIS: When?

RACHEL: Just now.

PHYLLIS: Oh. Oh yeah. You know Rachel…

RACHEL: Yeah?

PHYLLIS: I'm kinda scared.

RACHEL: How come?

PHYLLIS: I always feel scared when someone dies, 'cause then I know someone else is gonna die too. And with old Angus dying…

RACHEL: Is this that dying in three shit?

PHYLLIS: It's not shit.

RACHEL: Just Angus is dead. That's only one.

PHYLLIS: This time feels like three.

RACHEL: Aehhhh.

PHYLLIS: Sure.

RACHEL: Talk about something else.

PHYLLIS: So'd you hear about Margret?

RACHEL: What's that?

PHYLLIS: She's pregnant.

RACHEL: No way.

PHYLLIS: Sure.

RACHEL: Who told you then?

PHYLLIS: Nigger.

RACHEL: And how does he know?

PHYLLIS: I don't know. Maybe he did it.

RACHEL: As if he could even find it. So Teddy's gonna have another kid. What's that make...four? Ten?

PHYLLIS: That's just what I heard.

> (They now have enough tobacco for two cigarettes. RACHEL sniffs her fingers and then chops her hands together to cleanse them of any loose tobacco. PHYLLIS wipes her hands off on her pants.)

RACHEL: There. D'you got any rolling paper?

PHYLLIS: No. I thought you had some.

RACHEL: Fuck.

PHYLLIS: Maybe we could just burn it and wave the smoke into our mouths.

RACHEL: You can't taste it that way. What the hell good is tobacco if you can't taste it.

PHYLLIS: I don't know.

RACHEL: I don't know.

PHYLLIS: Well don't get mad at me. I don't need rolling papers. I just buy my cigrettes.

RACHEL: Well help me find something. Get some paper.

> (PHYLLIS exits.)

PHYLLIS: (Off.) How 'bout wax paper?

RACHEL:	We're not tryin' to make cookies.
PHYLLIS:	*(Entering.)* How 'bout toilet paper?
RACHEL:	We need something thin like that. Like rolling paper. I know.

> *(RACHEL exits and returns quickly. She's leafing through a Bible, looking for an acceptable page. PHYLLIS shrieks and immediately grabs the Bible. RACHEL doesn't let go.)*

PHYLLIS:	No. No way. You're not using that.
RACHEL:	What's wrong?
PHYLLIS:	No way. Not the Bible. It's bad luck.
RACHEL:	What? No it isn't.
PHYLLIS:	Yes. Yes it is. You can't. This is like a holy book. You can't use it to make cigrettes.
RACHEL:	Why?
PHYLLIS:	'Cause it's bad. It's bad luck. We'll get in an accident. Or you'll get cancer or something.
RACHEL:	It's just a book Phyllis. It's only words.
PHYLLIS:	The words of God.

> *(They have a slight tug of war.)*

RACHEL:	Let go. Let go. Phyllis.
PHYLLIS:	No. You can't use this.
RACHEL:	For fuck sakes Phyllis.
PHYLLIS:	You can't use this. *(PHYLLIS wrenches the Bible free.)* We got our names from this Bible.
RACHEL:	I don't think there was a Phyllis in the Bible.

> *(There's a loud thumping at the door. PHYLLIS charges to the door.)*

PHYLLIS:	Goddamn you kids…

(She opens the door and screams. NIGGER's standing there, propping himself against the door frame. His pant leg is torn and bloody.)

NIGGER: Ahneen Phyllis. Ahneen cousin.

(PHYLLIS stares at NIGGER's leg in shock. NIGGER gets hit in the head with a fishhead. He picks it up, falls, and throws it back. PHYLLIS screams out the door as she helps NIGGER up.)

PHYLLIS: You stupid kids. Quit throwing fishheads. Go play at the dump I said.

(RACHEL also helps.)

RACHEL: Holy shit. Nigger who beat you up this time?

(PHYLLIS and RACHEL sit NIGGER at the table. PHYLLIS goes into the kitchen.)

NIGGER: Meegwetch cousin.

RACHEL: Who beat you up? *(RACHEL looks at his leg and sucks in her breath.)*

NIGGER: Animush.

(PHYLLIS returns with some tea towels/rags and water. PHYLLIS cleans NIGGER's leg.)

RACHEL: Whose nickname is that?

PHYLLIS: Dog.

RACHEL: I know it's a dog.

NIGGER: No nickname, that's who bit me. *(NIGGER looks at the tobacco on the table.)* Hey, who wrecked these butts?

RACHEL: No one. We were gonna make cigrettes.

NIGGER: You should have just saved these for me. I smoke butts.

RACHEL: Take it.

NIGGER: Meegwetch. *(NIGGER takes the tobacco.)*

RACHEL: Why'd animush bite you?

NIGGER: The kids at the church were playing with him and they were trying to make him dance. They were picking him up like that and swingin' him around— (NIGGER mimes this.) and I went to stop them, and then that dog went wicked. And he chased me. And bit my leg.

RACHEL: Looks more like he chewed it.

(PHYLLIS bandages his leg.)

PHYLLIS: You're gonna need stitches Nigger.

NIGGER: Nahhh. Teach me right for trying to help a dog. Maybe dogs like to dance.

(ROBERT TRAVERSE, sits and watches satellite television. He runs "Rob's Plumbing", a septic and plumbing service which serves Partridge Crop and the surrounding reserves. He is dressed in expensive clothes, something one would find in Harry Rosen. He's changing through several channels rapidly, finding nothing in particular that he likes. There is a knock at the door. Without getting up, ROBERT calls out.)

ROBERT: Come in. If your nose is clean.

(MELVIN enters. He shakes his shoes and wipes them, making far too much of it.)

MELVIN: Can I take off my jacket?

ROBERT: Go ahead. Come in.

MELVIN: So. How are you doing?

ROBERT: I'm OK.

MELVIN: That's good. (MELVIN sits.) What are you watching?

ROBERT: Aaah. Nothing. There's nothing good on.

MELVIN: How 'bout wrestling? Is there any wrestling on?

ROBERT: Not tonight.

MELVIN: Right. Is there any good westerns on?

ROBERT: I don't know. Maybe.

             (ROBERT scans through some channels until he
             finds a western.)

             So what's on your mind Melvin?

MELVIN: I just came to visit. And watch satellite.

ROBERT: You seem like you want something though.

MELVIN: I wanted to ask you something.

ROBERT: Go ahead.

MELVIN: Were you thinking of running for chief?

ROBERT: Are you kidding? I can't run for chief. My business
             takes up all my time.

MELVIN: You could still run for chief though.

ROBERT: No. I don't know.

MELVIN: You should. You'd be a good chief.

ROBERT: Why do you say that?

MELVIN: Well. You uhhh… You got money. You dress nice.
             You've got a satellite. You're the only one around
             here with a job. We need a guy like you in the band
             office.

ROBERT: Thank you for saying that.

MELVIN: You could make this one of the richest reserves in
             Manitoba.

ROBERT: That could never happen.

MELVIN: You could make it happen.

ROBERT: This band is in a co-manager's agreement with
             Indian Affairs. It's been in receivership. That's like
             being bankrupt.

MELVIN:	See. You know all that stuff. I'll tell you what.
ROBERT:	What?
MELVIN:	I wanted to ask you something else.
ROBERT:	Go ahead.
MELVIN:	I've seen this one before. Is Jimmy Swaggart on there?
ROBERT:	I think so. Somewhere.
	(ROBERT scans the channels until he finds an evangelist.)
MELVIN:	This guy's good.
ROBERT:	So what else did you want to ask me?
MELVIN:	I wanted to ask…if you'll run for chief. I'll vote for you. I'll do that favour for you because I know that this reserve needs a guy like you in the band office. The only favour I ask is that you gimme five bucks for gas.
ROBERT:	I'm not running for chief.
MELVIN:	OK. OK. Maybe not now, but think it over. Maybe later you will.
ROBERT:	Maybe.
MELVIN:	So?
ROBERT:	What?
MELVIN:	Could I get five bucks off you? I just need enough to last me till my cheque comes.
ROBERT:	I don't do that sort of thing.
MELVIN:	You've got a pump right out there. Just lend me the key. All I want is some gas.
ROBERT:	That gas is for my trucks. I have to keep track of how much I've got.
MELVIN:	I know. You won't miss a little bit though. Maybe

ten dollars worth. Five. Five dollars worth.

ROBERT: I don't do that Melvin. I'll tell you what, come and see me on Monday. You can work for me, servicing the septic tanks. I have more work than workers.

MELVIN: I guess there's a lot of shit everywhere.

ROBERT: And I need guys like you to help me get rid of it. If you come to work for me I'll start you at seven dollars an hour.

MELVIN: Oh. Yeah? Wow. That much eh? Well, I'll have to think about that. For sure. Well, thanks a lot anyways Robert.

ROBERT: Alright. Come back another time maybe, for wrestling.

MELVIN: Yeah. Or a movie. I like that one, *Little Big Man*.

ROBERT: Yes. That's a good one.

MELVIN: OK. Well, I can't get five bucks off you eh? Goodnight. *(He gets up to leave.)* That's a nice new truck you got there. Did you just buy it?

ROBERT: Yes I did.

MELVIN: Oh. Well. See you.

ROBERT: Goodnight.

(ROBERT goes back to switching channels. MELVIN leaves.)

(Spotlight up on the case of beer sitting on TEDDY SINCLAIR's table. The room itself is a half kitchen, half living room, with no real division between the two. It is cluttered with all sorts of junk. TEDDY runs a pawnshop out of it. Other than this, it's fairly typical of any house of a "poorer" family on the reserve. Sitting at the table are TEDDY and NIGGER. TEDDY is averaged-sized, dressed in leather. He wears several rings, a choker and a gold necklace with an eagle pendant. They've both been drinking for some time and show the alcohol's effect.

NIGGER's suffering from a toothache. TEDDY finishes off a cigarette and butts it out. They're both playing poker.)

NIGGER: Oooooooo. Oh shit I need some medcin.

TEDDY: Here. Drink some more beer. *(TEDDY offers him a bottle.)*

NIGGER: No.

TEDDY: Just don't think about it then.

NIGGER: Well what'll I think about?

TEDDY: I don't know. Women.

NIGGER: Oooooooo. That stupid salmon from B.C. I chewed a bone I think. Owwwww.

TEDDY: Play poker.

    (NIGGER lays down his cards and looks at a fiddle hanging among the junk.)

NIGGER: I win my fiddle back.

TEDDY: Bullshit. I beat you.

NIGGER: Aweeenuk. No way, boy. Three of a kind beats two pair.

TEDDY: No. You lose. Two pair beats three of a kind. You need a full house or a straight to beat me. You owe me five bucks.

NIGGER: No way. You're cheating.

TEDDY: Bullshit. Go to Las Vegas. You'll see. I used to go with the chief all the time. I know how to play poker. So pay me my five bucks.

NIGGER: Here.

    (NIGGER takes off his hat and slams it on the table and immediately grabs his jaw.)

Ooooo. There, that's my hat from when I was on the DOTC.

TEDDY: You weren't on a Tribal Council.

NIGGER: No. We was the Dakota Ojibway Teepee Creepers. We were Manitoba Champs in 1970. I was goalie. I stopped lots of shots. I even took a slapshot in the head from Jim Beaulieau. And I didn't even wear a mask. That knocked out one of my tooths. *(NIGGER holds his face, having reminded himself that he has a toothache.)*

TEDDY: I don't want this stupid hat. Just owe me five bucks.

NIGGER: What kind of pawnshop do you have here. Won't even take stuff.

TEDDY: It's not a pawnshop. It's a storage place. I just charge you rent. That's all.

NIGGER: You're cheating from us.

TEDDY: Hey. At least I got a job. Don't tell me what's bad for our people. I don't see you doing anything.

                (TEDDY shuffles the cards. NIGGER takes the cigarette TEDDY butted out and straightens it.)

NIGGER: Got a light?

TEDDY: Why the hell do you do that?

NIGGER: I want a cigrette.

TEDDY: Don't take them out of the ashtray. Just ask for one.

NIGGER: Do you got a cigrette?

TEDDY: No.

NIGGER: Got a light then. Please?

                (TEDDY grabs a lighter which could have been found on coffee tables during the 1970s; it's an Inuit carving of a bear. TEDDY lights NIGGER's cigarette butt.)

NIGGER: Meegwetch. *(NIGGER takes as long a drag as the butt will last and then puts it out. He seems to enjoy it. Waits a bit and then contorts his face.)*

TEDDY: You better go see the dentist.

NIGGER: No way. All those guys are good for is pulling teeth. Can I borrow my fiddle back?

TEDDY: You got ten bucks?

NIGGER: I thought it was five.

TEDDY: You just lost five, plus five for the fiddle from before.

NIGGER: Owooooo. I'll pay you when I get my cheque tomorrow.

TEDDY: You can't even play the damn thing anyways.

NIGGER: Yessir. I can. I taught with Ed Desjarlais. He had a Stravarius from the priest at Sandy Bay. That fiddle he had was worth over a hunerd bucks.

TEDDY: And what did he do with it?

NIGGER: He hawked it for twenty-five. (*They both laugh.*) Oooouuuch.

TEDDY: Fuck sakes you're giving me a toothache. Use something to tie around your head.

NIGGER: What?

TEDDY: Use your belt or something to tie around your head.

NIGGER: What for?

TEDDY: That's what you do when you get a toothache.

NIGGER: My pants'll fall down.

TEDDY: Gimme your belt.

NIGGER: No. Wait.

> (*NIGGER reluctantly removes his belt, and his pants fall down. NIGGER ties the belt around the top of his head, like a headband.*)

TEDDY: You're worse than an old woman. Never mind. Let's see your sock.

NIGGER: No.

(TEDDY grabs NIGGER's leg and lifts it. NIGGER screams in pain.)

NIGGER: Owww. My leg's still sore.

TEDDY: That'll teach you to tease dogs. You're lucky they didn't chew off your whole damn leg.

NIGGER: That one dog was a wolf I think.

TEDDY: No way. That was just Robert's dog. That dog's too stupid to be a wolf.

(TEDDY lifts up NIGGER's pants in order to remove NIGGER's sock. Marvelling at NIGGER's damaged leg.)

Holy shit. He took a chunk out of your leg. I'll have to go shoot that dog for you.

NIGGER: That's not where Cecil's dog bit me. That's where that chainsaw fell on my leg that time. Boy that hurt. This one here is where those dogs bit me. No. No. Wait. That's not where I got bit. That's from that time I accidently shot myself with my .22. That one didn't hurt so bad.

(TEDDY removes NIGGER's sock. It's a long white tube sock that's quite soiled and closer to grey with black highlights. TEDDY removes it. NIGGER's foot is dirty.)

TEDDY: You should wash your feet boy. They stink.

NIGGER: I should get you to wash them for me.

TEDDY: Fuck that. (TEDDY attempts to tie the sock around NIGGER's head.) This sock smells funny.

NIGGER: I'll buy a new one tomorrow. Owooooooo. Don't tie that around my head. That'll be like I'm dead.

TEDDY: What?

NIGGER: That's what I had to do when my dad died that time. He was like this. (NIGGER lays his head back *with his jaw open.)* And I had to tie a cloth there to close his mouth. That'll be like I'm dead.

TEDDY: So?

(NIGGER thinks and then lets TEDDY proceed. TEDDY ties the sock around NIGGER's head. NIGGER waits and then grimaces.)

NIGGER: Uuuuhhhh.

TEDDY: *(Picks up a shoe with laces.)* Here. Let's see your tooth.

NIGGER: What're you gonna do?

TEDDY: Open your mouth.

(NIGGER does so.)

You got bad breath man.

NIGGER: Must be all that salmon samich.

TEDDY: Which one is it?

NIGGER: The black one.

TEDDY: They're all black.

NIGGER: The black one with the hole.

TEDDY: Is it this one? *(TEDDY inserts his finger. Prodding each tooth until he hits the jackpot. NIGGER bites him.)* Owwch.

(TEDDY tries to tie one end of the shoe's laces to NIGGER's tooth.)

Open your mouth more.

NIGGER: *(His mouth open.)* I can't. What're you gonna do?

TEDDY: I'm gonna tie this to your tooth and then I'll just pull on this like a skidoo. *(He holds up the shoe.)* Open your mouth more.

NIGGER: *(His mouth open.)* I can't.

(TEDDY tries to tie the lace to NIGGER's tooth, fails, and throws the shoe down.)

TEDDY: Shit.

NIGGER: I'll just go see old Walter tomorrow. He'll do some
                medcin for me.

TEDDY: He doesn't know any medicine.

                *(TEDDY gets up, goes to the drawer and removes
                pliers.)*

NIGGER: Sure he does. He healed my 'monia that time.

TEDDY: Yeah. Bullshit. I'll fix your tooth.

                *(He returns to the table. Holds NIGGER's jaw and
                then he tries to insert the pliers into his mouth.)*

NIGGER: Wait. Wait.

TEDDY: This'll just hurt a bit.

NIGGER: OK. OK. Wait.

                *(NIGGER lays his head back and opens his mouth as
                wide as he can. TEDDY inserts the pliers.)*

TEDDY: Open your mouth more.

NIGGER: *(Mouth open.)* I can't.

                *(TEDDY pulls. NIGGER's head gets yanked back
                and forth a few times.)*

TEDDY: Shit. Here. Let me try again.

NIGGER: No.

TEDDY: If I don't you're gonna have to suffer.

NIGGER: Ahh that's OK. I'm used to it.

                (TEDDY throws down the pliers.)

TEDDY: Wait I know. Here. Lie down.

NIGGER: OK. *(He lies down.)*

TEDDY: OK. Wait. *(TEDDY straddles NIGGER and sits on his
                stomach. He then rolls up his sleeves. He makes a fist and
                cocks his arm.)*

NIGGER: Wait. Wait. What're you doing?

TEDDY: I'll just punch your tooth out. It won't hurt that much.

NIGGER: Wait. Wait. Get me some more beer. I need a sip of that first.

> (TEDDY gets NIGGER a beer. He quaffs it, and stalls some more by drinking another. TEDDY grabs the beer from him.)

NIGGER: OK. OK. Wait.

> (NIGGER lies still and turns his cheek, offering TEDDY a better target. TEDDY grabs NIGGER's jaw and turns his face towards him. He cocks his fist.)

TEDDY: This'll only hurt a bit.

NIGGER: Can I borrow my fiddle after?

> (Lights out. A smack sound. NIGGER moans.)

> (The next afternoon. The scene opens on "Walter's", the restaurant/coffee shop/convenience store/gas station of the Partridge Crop Reserve. There is a booth-like table, a full ashtray on it. MELVIN sits at the table. He sips coffee. RACHEL and PHYLLIS walk in.)

PHYLLIS: Just wait a sec I wannu cash this cheque.

RACHEL: What cheque?

PHYLLIS: I went to the band office last week 'cause one of my kids needs new shoes. (PHYLLIS calls into the back of the store.) Walter, can you cash this cheque for me? Where the hell is Walter?

> (RACHEL takes the cheque looks at it and gives it back to her.)

RACHEL: That's a bad cheque. Don't bother.

PHYLLIS: Why not? It's from the band office.

RACHEL: That's exactly why. It's no good.

PHYLLIS:	Sure it's good.

(RACHEL *walks over to* MELVIN *and sits down.* PHYLLIS *waits for a bit before sitting with* MELVIN *and* RACHEL.)

RACHEL:	Hey.
MELVIN:	Hi.
PHYLLIS:	What's the matter with you?
MELVIN:	Nothing.
RACHEL:	So where's Teddy and those guys?
MELVIN:	I don't know. They're probably partying.
RACHEL:	And you're not with them?
PHYLLIS:	Would you cash my cheque for me Melvin?
MELVIN:	I don't got any money. Ask Teddy. And I don't party with those guys anymore.
RACHEL:	Oh yeah. That's right. You're a Christian now eh?
MELVIN:	So'd the cheques come yet?
PHYLLIS:	Nah. Later. They said they'll come this afternoon.
MELVIN:	That's good.
PHYLLIS:	No it isn't I need money now.
MELVIN:	So does everybody.
RACHEL:	What's wrong with you?
MELVIN:	Nothing.
RACHEL:	I know what you mean.

(ROBERT *enters.*)

ROBERT:	Have any of you seen Walter?
RACHEL:	Nope.
PHYLLIS:	Hey Robert. Excuse me.

MELVIN:	Don't bother Phyllis.
PHYLLIS:	Could you do me a favour?
ROBERT:	What's that?
PHYLLIS:	Could you cash my cheque for me?
ROBERT:	*(Shakes his head.)* Sorry. I don't do that sort of thing. So Melvin, have you thought about what we discussed?
MELVIN:	I need a bit more time.
ROBERT:	You let me know. And please tell Walter I want to settle my account with him.

> *(ROBERT leaves. NIGGER walks in quickly, hobbling. He has news to tell, but first he picks up a Pepsi, bag of chips, a bar and a handful of Bazooka Joe bubblegum. He has a black eye and is missing one of his front teeth. The sock is still tied around his head.)*

NIGGER:	Boy Walter, are these Bazooka Joe's on sale?

> *(NIGGER walks over to the other three at the table. NIGGER digs through the ashtray on the table and pockets several butts.)*

Hey you guys, how's it goin'?

PHYLLIS:	Alright.
RACHEL:	What's the hell happened to you anyways? And how come you got a sock on your head?
NIGGER:	I was getting my tooth out.
RACHEL:	Good dentist. Gimme a zip. *(NIGGER passes her the Pepsi, she returns it after taking a sip.)* Thanks.
NIGGER:	So'd our fareWel cheques come yet?
PHYLLIS:	They don't come till later.

> *(NIGGER opens everything, and starts to eat very gently, trying not to hurt his tooth. PHYLLIS starts sniffing the air.)*

Do you guys smell tacos? I smell tacos.

MELVIN: That's 'cause he's eating them.

NIGGER: No. These are barbeque. *(He eats some chips.)* So'd you guys hear about Schmidty?

PHYLLIS: No. What?

NIGGER: He got killed.

PHYLLIS: No.

RACHEL: What?

MELVIN: When?

NIGGER: Just a little while ago.

PHYLLIS: I knew it.

RACHEL: Where?

NIGGER: On Number Six, by Moosehorn.

MELVIN: Holy shit.

RACHEL: What happened?

NIGGER: He went in the ditch or something. I think they said he lost control.

PHYLLIS: Poor Schmidty. Poor Schmidty. I knew it. I knew it. That's two now.

RACHEL: Holy shit.

PHYLLIS: That's two. There's gonna be one more now.

RACHEL: Shut up Phyllis.

MELVIN: Did he hit another car?

NIGGER: I don't know. I just heard it from Jim Sinclair.

RACHEL: Who found him?

NIGGER: I don't know.

PHYLLIS: Oh Jesus.

MELVIN:	Was he drunk?
NIGGER:	Probly. That's pretty shitty eh? (*He offers his chips to RACHEL.*)
RACHEL:	Would you fuck off with that. You come in here to tell us Schmidty's dead and you start eating. You didn't even tell us that first. You asked about our fuckin' welfare cheques. That's all this reserve cares about anymore. Welfare and partying.
NIGGER:	I didn't know. Jim Sinclair just told me.
MELVIN:	How old was he anyways?
PHYLLIS:	Twenty-five I think. Jesus.
RACHEL:	He was twenty-two.

(*TEDDY, hung-over, enters and walks to the table.*)

PHYLLIS:	Hey Teddy did you hear about Schmidty?
TEDDY:	What, is he dead?
PHYLLIS:	How did you know?
TEDDY:	Whenever someone asks me if I've heard about anyone, they're either pregnant or dead.
RACHEL:	You know everything eh?
TEDDY:	I know more than you. (*He lights up a cigarette.*) Do you want one? (*He offers one to RACHEL.*)

(*NIGGER takes one of the butts he removed from the ashtray out of his pocket.*)

RACHEL:	I quit.
TEDDY:	Oh yeah.

(*TEDDY takes a drag and blows the smoke in RACHEL's direction.*)

NIGGER:	Got a light?

(*TEDDY lights NIGGER's cigarette butt. It's good for about half a drag. PHYLLIS gets up.*)

PHYLLIS: We gotta go see Schmidty's granny. *(She starts to leave and then stops.)* Can you cash my cheque for me Teddy?

TEDDY: Sure. But I charge ten bucks.

PHYLLIS: Oh that's OK.

               (PHYLLIS hands him the cheque. TEDDY takes it and simultaneously begins to remove his wallet. He looks at the cheque and then hands it back to her as he puts his wallet back.)

TEDDY: Forget it.

PHYLLIS: Oh. You coming Rachel?

NIGGER: Well. There it is eh. Schmidty's number two. Death always comes in three. Last week, old Angus. And now Schmidty. I hope he has a good trip.

RACHEL: What?

MELVIN: He means he hopes he went to heaven.

NIGGER: No I don't.

TEDDY: So I guess there's gonna be a job at the band office now.

RACHEL: Why don't you shut up.

TEDDY: Why don't you stop acting like you give a shit. You're just doing that for everyone else.

RACHEL: I cared more about him than you did.

TEDDY: Go home and make some pies for the wake then.

MELVIN: *(Sniffing.)* I smell tacos too now.

RACHEL: Shut up Melvin.

TEDDY: You shut up Rachel. Did you know Schmidty thought you were a fat bitch.

PHYLLIS: Let's go Rachel.

               (RACHEL gets up and leaves with PHYLLIS.)

TEDDY:	That took a little longer than usual.
MELVIN:	So what happened to your eye Nigger? Were you in a fight?
NIGGER:	I told you. I was getting my tooth out.
MELVIN:	Through your eye?
NIGGER:	No. It's a new way. You punch it out. Just like that. *(He mimes punching TEDDY in the jaw.)*
MELVIN:	If you wanted to beat him up you should have just fought him.
TEDDY:	I would never fight Nigger. He's like a father-in-law to me.
MELVIN:	So how come you got a sock on your head?
NIGGER:	That's what you do when you got a sore tooth. I still might go find Walter though. Teddy didn't get the right one.
MELVIN:	You don't need Indian medicine, Nigger. They'd pray for you at church.
NIGGER:	Nah. All that church is good for is wakes.
	(NIGGER offers everyone a piece of Bazooka Joe. Only MELVIN takes some. NIGGER reads the comic.)
TEDDY:	I should put my name in for Schmidty's job.
MELVIN:	Let him get cold first Teddy.
TEDDY:	You gotta move fast man. I'm just being real. He's dead. And that's bad. I mean I liked that little asshole you know. He was good to drink with. But I'm just saying that life goes on eh? Someone's gonna get his job. It should be me. Too bad it couldn't be you.
MELVIN:	It could be me.
TEDDY:	No it can't. You're Bill C-31. Only real Indians can work for the band.

MELVIN: I'm a real Indian.

NIGGER: *(Reading the comic.)* "My man, Jay flyin', then I see a gross one Mason." *(He laughs.)*

MELVIN: What?

NIGGER: "My man, Jane vlyin then I see. Gross. Or one Mason." *(He laughs again.)*

MELVIN: What the hell are you reading?

NIGGER: That's Bazooka Joe and his gang. He's talking to his friend Jay in that one. I like that little guy with the scarf on his face all the time. Like he's gonna rob a bank.

MELVIN: Maybe he's a doctor.

TEDDY: Gimme that. *(He takes the comic and reads it with great difficulty.)* "Ma, I saw a dog as big as a house. Pesty must you eggsagerate? I've told you a million times." *(He turns it over as if he were looking for a better punchline.)*

NIGGER: That wasn't funny. You read it wrong.

MELVIN: Let's see. *(TEDDY gives it to him.)* "Maman, j'ai vliun chen aussi…" That's French, Nigger, you asshole.

TEDDY: Don't read that shit around here.

NIGGER: How come they got French on Bazooka Joe?

TEDDY: Because, this is Canada.

(The next day. The scene opens on a queue with RACHEL at the front. There is a window, which is closed. Behind her stands PHYLLIS and NIGGER, who still has the sock on his head, and a stick under his arm. They are all waiting for their welfare cheques.)

PHYLLIS: Where are they already?

RACHEL: Just relax. They said they'd be here.

PHYLLIS: How come you got that stick Nigger?

NIGGER: It's my crotch.

RACHEL: Crutch.

NIGGER: Yeah. I found it in the bush. I need it to walk and in case that wicked dog comes to bite me. I'll hit him with this. Just like my dad hit my dog. Except he had a two by four that time. Mooshabay. That was my dog. And he was chewing the laundry that time and my dad was fixing his nets. And he picked up a two by four and hit my dog on the head. And then he threw him on the wagon for the dump 'cause he was dead. Boy, three days later that dog comes back. His head all like this. (*NIGGER does his best impression of Mooshabay's busted head.*) We kept that dog after that too. He lived long.

PHYLLIS: What do you think happens to Schmidty's cheque?

RACHEL: He had a job. He never got a cheque from here.

PHYLLIS: Oh. Poor Schmidty.

NIGGER: (*Pulling a butt out of his pocket.*) You guys got a light?

             (*RACHEL pulls out a lighter and lights NIGGER's smoke.*)

RACHEL: I'll give you cigrettes after I get my cheque. You shouldn't pick up butts. What'd you do with all that tobacco we gave you?

NIGGER: I smoked it.

RACHEL: Where'd you get rolling paper?

NIGGER: I just used a Bible and jam.

PHYLLIS: That's bad Nigger. Something bad's gonna happen to you.

NIGGER: Maybe I'm next.

RACHEL: For what?

NIGGER: To die.

PHYLLIS: I told you Rachel. I told you. I knew this time felt like three.

RACHEL: Be quiet.

NIGGER: That time the Sumner's baby died, and then old Jack Sinclair died and then I got sick. I thought for sure it was me. I was gonna die. Number three. That time I had 'monia in my heart. I thought for sure I was gonna die.

RACHEL: Would you guys shut up.

PHYLLIS: I don't want to be three Rachel. We shouldn'tna almost smoked that Bible. I don't like this. I don't feel good feelings about this. Would you get my cheque for me Rachel?

RACHEL: No. You get your own cheque. You're just embarrassed to get it.

PHYLLIS: No. I'm scared. Please?

(MELVIN enters.)

MELVIN: *(Singing.)* ...fareWel in the family, happy, happy day. FareWel in the family, happy, happy day. *(Noticing everyone in line.)* Holy shit. What. Do you guys camp out overnight here or something?

RACHEL: Shut up Melvin. You're here too.

MELVIN: I'm just kidding.

PHYLLIS: Melvin, would you get my cheque for me?

MELVIN: Sorry mama. No can do.

(RACHEL walks closer to MELVIN and looks at him.)

PHYLLIS: Would you get my cheque for me Nigger?

NIGGER: I'm already getting Teddy's. What the hell's taking so long.

(RACHEL slaps MELVIN. MELVIN grabs her.)

MELVIN: Hey. You stupid bitch.

RACHEL: Quit sniffing gas you asshole.

(*MELVIN lets go of RACHEL.*)

MELVIN: I wasn't.

RACHEL: Why are your lips blue then?

MELVIN: Why the hell do you care?

RACHEL: You quit sniffing. OK?

PHYLLIS: You should try harder to be a Christian Melvin. Christians don't sniff.

NIGGER: That sniffing's no good. I caught fire the time I tried it.

MELVIN: That's 'cause you're not supposed to smoke and sniff at the same time. (*Sings.*) FareWel in the family, happy, happy home. FareWel in the family, happy, happy home.

RACHEL: I hate this place.

(*They wait. Tableaus of them as time passes, the whole day. RACHEL starts to leave.*)

PHYLLIS: Where are you going?

RACHEL: Back to Winnipeg.

PHYLLIS: Why?

RACHEL: To live.

PHYLLIS: What? Wait. Don't go. The cheques'll be here soon.

RACHEL: You can have mine. I've had enough.

PHYLLIS: Rachel wait.

(*RACHEL leaves. NIGGER begins banging on the window.*)

NIGGER: Heyyyy. (*He begins banging harder.*) What the hell is going on? Heyyyyy.

MELVIN: Heyyy. Heyyy. Heyyayyayyayy. Heyyayyayyayy.

(*MELVIN begins to dance, slowly.*)

PHYLLIS: Shit. See. Now all this bad stuff's happening. How
                am I supposed to feed my kids? (*PHYLLIS moves to
                the window and begins hitting it.*) Heyy. Open up. I
                need my money.

                (*MELVIN continues to dance. PHYLLIS tries to
                pry the window open with her hands. Eventually
                they start pushing each other.*)

                I'm getting my cheque. I need my cheque. (*In
                desperation, she tries with all that she has, to open the
                window. It doesn't give. She gives up, crying.*) I need
                my cheque. How am I gonna feed my kids? I'm
                gonna go to the chief's house and take one of his
                cows.

NIGGER: He's in Vegas.

                (*PHYLLIS grabs NIGGER's stick and hits the
                window with it. The stick breaks.*)

PHYLLIS: My kid's'll starve. What the hell are we supposed to
                eat?

                (*MELVIN's dancing has reached a lethargic peak.
                He stops and raises his hands in the air.*)

MELVIN: Happy day.

                (*Lights come up on Walter's Restaurant. Several
                hours have passed. There are some arranged chairs,
                awaiting an audience. A box is being used as a
                podium. There are some crude signs with pictures of
                TEDDY on them. NIGGER hobbles towards the
                counter and uses whatever he can to prop himself
                up.*)

NIGGER: Hey Walter. Walter. Where the hell are you? I need
                some medcin. Fix my tooth for me. And my leg too.
                Where the hell is Walter?

                (*TEDDY enters.*)

TEDDY: OK. Come sit over here. (*He motions to the chairs.*)

NIGGER: I can't walk good.

TEDDY:	Be a man eh?

(NIGGER hobbles over to the chairs.)

NIGGER: Ooo. Aahh. Ooo. Aah.

(He sits down.)

What's this anyways?

TEDDY: It's a meeting. You'll see when Melvin and them get here.

(ROBERT walks in.)

Shit.

NIGGER: What?

TEDDY: We don't need this asshole.

ROBERT: Walter? Walter? Teddy have you seen Walter?

TEDDY: Nope.

(ROBERT walks behind the counter and pulls out a little book.)

ROBERT: Tell him I came to pay my bill. *(ROBERT looks in the book and puts a cheque in it.)* Nine hunerd bucks. Man. Man. Those kids'll make me go broke. Tell Walter not to let my kids charge burgers and stuff on here again unless I say it's OK. Alright?

TEDDY: Tell him yourself.

(MELVIN walks in.)

Where's Cheezie and Rudy and those guys. I told you to bring them.

MELVIN: Cheezie's passed out and those other guys went to Little Sask for bingo.

TEDDY: For fuck sakes.

ROBERT: So Melvin, when are you coming to work for me?

MELVIN: Uhh...

TEDDY:	He's gonna work for me.
ROBERT:	Doing what?
TEDDY:	I don't know yet.

(RACHEL walks in quickly with a duffel bag. She's followed closely by PHYLLIS.)

PHYLLIS:	Don't go. I'll be lonesome.
RACHEL:	Walter. Walter. Is that guy ever here?
TEDDY:	Going somewhere Rachel?
RACHEL:	None of your business. Where the hell is Walter?
PHYLLIS:	Don't go. You don't have money to buy a bus ticket anyways.
RACHEL:	I'll pay Walter back.

(TEDDY removes his wallet and offers RACHEL some money.)

TEDDY:	Here.
RACHEL:	Get out of here Teddy. I don't want your money.
TEDDY:	You were gonna take it before.
RACHEL:	When?
TEDDY:	That time. In Winnipeg.
RACHEL:	You're so slack Teddy.
PHYLLIS:	Our welfare will come Rachel. Don't leave just 'cause of that.
RACHEL:	It's not 'cause of that Phyllis. It's 'cause this place'll never get any better...fuck, forget it.
ROBERT:	What's this about the welfare?
PHYLLIS:	Rachel...
RACHEL:	I'll see you later.

(PHYLLIS tries to sit. TEDDY stops her.)

TEDDY:	Get lost Phyllis. Take off with your friend there. No women allowed here, at this meeting.
ROBERT:	What meeting? What's going on? Someone talk to me.
TEDDY:	We're having a meeting on self-government.

(RACHEL stops at the door and drops her bag. ROBERT laughs.)

	What the hell's so funny?
ROBERT:	This is about self-government?
TEDDY:	Yeah.
RACHEL:	Whose self-government?
TEDDY:	Ours. The Partridge Crop First Nation's.
PHYLLIS:	You wanna talk about self-government.
TEDDY:	I'm doing it. No more talking. There's been too much of that already.
RACHEL:	You can't do this.
TEDDY:	Watch me.
NIGGER:	Teddy's gonna get our fareWel back for us.
ROBERT:	What?
NIGGER:	They didn't have our fareWel cheques today. No happy day. It was sad day today.
ROBERT:	They're probably late. They'll come tomorrow.
TEDDY:	No more tomorrow. No more waiting. It's time we took control of our own money. No more fuckin' fareWel.
ROBERT:	The chief isn't gonna like this.
TEDDY:	He doesn't care. If he did he would have got our cheques for us. He's not even here.
ROBERT:	Where is he?

ALL: *(Save ROBERT.)* He's in Vegas.

ROBERT: Oh. Nobody told me.

RACHEL: So how do you suppose to do this?

TEDDY: We'll have nominations and then pick the chief. The new chief. I call this meeting to order. You guys sit down.

              (MELVIN, and PHYLLIS all move to sit down. RACHEL moves to stand at the back. ROBERT stands. TEDDY stops the women.)

              Not you.

RACHEL: Get out of here.

TEDDY: We don't need women in this political process. Get going to Winnipeg already. Good riddance.

PHYLLIS: Let's go Rachel.

RACHEL: No.

TEDDY: Leave.

RACHEL: You leave. Leave us alone. You're just gonna make things worse.

TEDDY: Look around you. Things can't get much worse. These people are gonna starve if I don't do something.

RACHEL: No one asked you to.

TEDDY: You're just trying to disrupt us here. Go on. Get going to Winnipeg.

RACHEL: Start your damn meeting already. I'm not leaving.

TEDDY: You don't get a vote.

ROBERT: You should at least listen to her Teddy.

TEDDY: I call this meeting to order.

ROBERT: By whose authority?

TEDDY:	My own.
ROBERT:	Are you the chair?
TEDDY:	Yes.
NIGGER:	Maybe he's a table.
TEDDY:	Quiet Nigger. Who nominates me?
ROBERT:	Hold it Teddy. You should be chosen chair first. And someone has to second that nomination. But you should have the selection of chair first.
TEDDY:	That's white man's ways.
RACHEL:	The whole thing you're doing is white man's ways. We never used to vote for chief.
TEDDY:	And women weren't allowed.
ROBERT:	Hold it. Hold it. You guys can't do this. You need to talk about this. Consultation. Consideration. More talk.
TEDDY:	That's all we've been doing is talk. It's time for action.
ROBERT:	You need to consult the Elders. Like Sheldon here.
TEDDY:	Consult. Talk. We do it. Now.
PHYLLIS:	Help us.
ROBERT:	This is a waste of time.
TEDDY:	If that's what you think self-government is, get the hell out. And take this stupid...troublemaker with you.

(ROBERT waits and is about to leave.)

MELVIN:	You'd be a good chief Robert.
TEDDY:	Shut up you little asshole.
ROBERT:	Go ahead Teddy.
TEDDY:	What?

ROBERT: Have someone nominate you.

(TEDDY hits NIGGER.)

NIGGER: Oh. I nominate Teddy Sinclair for thief. I mean chief. I nominate Teddy for chief.

ROBERT: Good. Now someone has to second you, or else you can't stand.

NIGGER: Why? Does he have to sit down?

ROBERT: You. Melvin. Do you second Teddy for chief?

MELVIN: I do.

ROBERT: OK. Well?

MELVIN: Well what?

ROBERT: Say, "I second Teddy for Chief."

MELVIN: Oh. I second Teddy for chief.

NIGGER: I third him.

ROBERT: You can't do that.

NIGGER: Why?

ROBERT: You don't have to. Now you have to have other nominations for the same position.

MELVIN: I nominate Robert Traverse for chief.

RACHEL: I second it.

TEDDY: You don't have a vote.

RACHEL: I second it.

ROBERT: Thank you, but I don't want to be chief. I'll help, but please don't nominate me. I'm not standing.

NIGGER: Standing. Sitting. Chairs. Tables. First. Second. How come Robert knows so much. I bet he's just lying to us.

ROBERT: I'm not lying to you. Look it up. I'm using *Robert's Rules of Order.*

NIGGER:	Aaaahhh. See. I knew it. These are his rules. He's just trying to get what he wants.
ROBERT:	I don't want anything. These rules aren't mine.
NIGGER:	Why are they called Robert's rules then?
ROBERT:	I don't know. Because that's who wrote them.
NIGGER:	Aaaahhh. He's lying. He wrote them.
TEDDY:	Let's get on with this.
NIGGER:	We're supposed to sing *O Canada* before our meeting or *God Safe the Queen*. *(Singing.)* "O Canada. Our home and native land..."—*(He punches up "native" for added effect.)* A Native person wrote that song.
MELVIN:	That's not what it means.
NIGGER:	Sure it does. Native. That's us right.
MELVIN:	Yeah, but not like that.
TEDDY:	I close the nominations and disbar Robert from running for chief.
NIGGER:	I second that.
PHYLLIS:	You guys can't do that.
RACHEL:	You can't be the only one running for chief. Robert's right. You don't even know what you're doing Teddy.
TEDDY:	I know what I'm doing. I'm getting things done finally. And I'm making things better for us.
RACHEL:	How? By doing the same damn thing as we got already. Self-government my ass. You're just calling it a different name. Trying to keep us women out of it. Not listening to anybody.
TEDDY:	OK. Let's vote now.
ROBERT:	Hey. Hey. Teddy. If you want this to be fair you should have a few more nominees. Running unopposed doesn't look good.

PHYLLIS: I nominate Melvin.

TEDDY
& RACHEL: I second.

TEDDY: I second him.

RACHEL: I do.

ROBERT: You guys. You guys. This isn't how you do it.

NIGGER: How do you know?

ROBERT: Because I've been to meetings. I know how to do this. Be quiet. Look. Listen. You need a secretary. You need more people. You can't do this the way you're doing it. Planning. Preparation. You need all of these things. These things have to be thought out.

TEDDY: Why?

ROBERT: Aww hell I'm leaving. You people are hopeless.

MELVIN: *(Stopping him.)* Wait. Robert you have to help us.

ROBERT: No one's listening to me. We can't do this. This doesn't mean anything. There's a procedure for valid elections. This isn't it.

TEDDY: Let him go.

MELVIN: Just stay.

ROBERT: There's no use. This isn't gonna work. We have to know what we're doing first. You need an understanding of procedure. You need bylaws. A constitution. Definitions.

TEDDY: We can learn all that as we go along.

ROBERT: No. You can't Teddy. We're only going to have one chance at self-government. If we're lucky.

RACHEL: And when have we ever been lucky? Just slow down a bit Teddy.

TEDDY: All this is is more talking. Time to vote.

PHYLLIS: Wait. Wait. I wanna pray first.

TEDDY:	No.
PHYLLIS:	Come on. I'm not nominated for anything. We need to pray first. Our people need God if we're gonna have self-government.
TEDDY:	Our people need our own beliefs. Not that whiteman bullshit religion.
NIGGER:	We need to sing *O Canada*.

> *(PHYLLIS starts to pray. Eventually everyone except TEDDY and RACHEL bows their head.)*

PHYLLIS:	Oh God, bless us in this thing we're doing, and don't let us be failures. And thank you for giving us Robert who can tell us what to do. And let our leaders be right and good for our people. Thank you Jesus. I don't know what self-government is, or what it's gonnu be, but I pray you'll help us in it. Thank you Jesus. And I'm sorry that we almost smoked your Bible and that nothing will happen to Rachel for that. Or to me. And don't let there be a number three. And bless Nigger, our Elder, and Melvin, and Teddy. And Lord maybe this isn't the time for us to have self-government, maybe we should wait for—
TEDDY:	Amen.
PHYLLIS:	Amen. Jesus. Amen. OK, now someone has to go and give a speech. You go Melvin.
MELVIN:	No. I want Robert to talk first. I'm not gonna talk. I just want to hear what he has to say.

> *(RACHEL begins to clap, chanting "Talk". Soon, everyone but TEDDY joins in, until ROBERT begins to talk.)*

ROBERT:	Listen. Self-government is something Native people should have had long ago. Instead of begging for handouts. Whether it's for our schools, our children or food. A lot of us who don't think we are, are really bums.
NIGGER:	That's me. I was a bum on Main street until that

police car hit me and I got ten thousand bucks and I came home, and then I sobered up.

ROBERT: I didn't mean you Nigger. I was just trying to make a point. I'm sorry if I offended you.

NIGGER: No. That's OK. I know who I am, and what I was. Just let me say something. The way I used to get money from people on the street was when I looked really pitiful. That's what you guys do when you go to Ottawa. Look really sad and they'll give you money. *(NIGGER makes a pitiful face.)* Or else play music. Like a fiddle. I'm gonna take my fiddle and go back to Winnipeg and make money.

ROBERT: This is supposed to be a meeting. A meeting on self-government. What is that? Can any of you tell me? Teddy. You tell me.

TEDDY: It's self-government. Just like the words mean. We govern ourselves. No more Indian Affairs.

ROBERT: How does it work?

TEDDY: Well...we get our own money. Instead of those assholes taking it. And we get to look after ourselves.

ROBERT: So what you're saying is, self-government is getting our own money. And looking after ourselves.

TEDDY: Yeah.

ROBERT: So then how do you deal with the fact that the Partridge Crop Reserve is broke. Their cheques all bounce. There's only one bank in Ashern that will cash welfare cheques and only welfare cheques. No other reserve cheques.

PHYLLIS: Teddy wouldn't even cash my little cheque.

ROBERT: Quiet Phyllis. Another question. Where is all this money going to come from to run your self-government?

TEDDY: The government.

ROBERT: And who gives them money?

TEDDY:	I don't care.
ROBERT:	Taxpayers. They can't even pay for Medicare anymore. And almost everything else. And that's for white people. You think they're gonna care about a bunch of Indians?
TEDDY:	They owe us.
ROBERT:	I know they do. But you live on what they've given you. The land on this reserve is all we're ever gonna get. This reserve is less than a thousand square miles. And this country is millions of square miles. But this is all we're gonna get. And we're gonna get even less, as the money runs out.
TEDDY:	We'll just take our land back.
RACHEL:	We can't. We lost it. We're a defeated nation.
ROBERT:	No. No we're not a defeated nation. We never were. That's the problem. If they came here and kicked our asses instead of shaking our hands everything would have been fine. At that time our people could understand defeat. What it is to lose a war. And what that means. Instead we get tricked. And all this shit you see around you is because of that. They're still tricking us. What do you think fareWel is?
TEDDY:	This guy's full of shit.
RACHEL:	Listen Teddy.
ROBERT:	Well Teddy?
TEDDY:	Well what?
ROBERT:	Is that all self-government is?
RACHEL:	No. It has to be more than that. We need to know what we're doing. We have to stop sitting around getting drunk, or sniffing gas, or trying to make ourselves rich without caring about anybody else. It used to be different. We took care of each other, and our children. That's why I want to leave, because in the city you know how it is. No one gives

a shit, but here...I know how it's supposed to be. And it isn't. We need to go back to the way it used to be. Like how people used to go from house to house at Christmas sharing food. And stories. We took care of each other. We listened. Remember Nigger?

(NIGGER can't. TEDDY stands on the box.)

TEDDY: Alright. Enough. I've listened to all of you and everybody's saying don't do it. We can't have self-government.

ROBERT: I said we need to know what it is first. And we shouldn't be changing things when our people aren't ready for it.

RACHEL: Just listen Teddy—

TEDDY: No. I know what we need.

(ROBERT leaves, shaking his head.)

Dih na way mahg a nay duk— (My friends and relatives—)

MELVIN: Wait, Teddy. Speak English.

TEDDY: Dih na way mahg a nay duk, asa wasa ki bi isha min ooma ka ai ing. Mi ooma ka dasi wo big ai ing. Ki kee asha dis oomin, shigo noong-um aa michi pee ang oki ma wi win chi meeni nang shoonian. A pee woogi mak an wi an ka ween shig o da ashan di seem. Kakina awiah ta meena shoonian. Ki ka meeni ni nim shoonia. A way woogi mah kan ka ishad Las Vegas, pi san igoo mas kowi see win ki woo ta bi namin. A pee das ta gooshing ki ka sagichi wa binanan, omah woo chi ish koon i ganing. Ki ka machi a tad i minoma. Kakina oona a tagaa wi nan ta pisco wheels of fortune, blackjack, shig oh slot machines. Mi ih kaa ishi shoonia kaa ing. Keena wind ki ga woono dah min awa naan ki anishinabaywid. Ka ween a woshi may ongo blond hair ka ahwad, shi go ka ay kawabi jee wabiwad Bill C-31 ka inid oh, ka pi woo ta pin a wad ki shoonia min nin. Shi go ka iah way anishinabaa wit tau win. Ki ka woo tabi na min iway koy ak anamiahwin. Ka ween a wooshi may owoo wa miti goo ishi woo dana mi way igamik. *(PHYLLIS shakes her head.)* Ka keena Bazooka Joes ta anishinabe wooshi pee i gaday. *(TEDDY holds up a Bazooka Joe comic.)* Keena wah ka kin ah ki masi na a ma wim ka goo. Phyllis ki masi na amau a shoonia. Nigger, ki masi na neen ka ki woo tabi na man ki wee bid.

(My friends and relatives, we have come far in our lives. We have lived here all of our lives. We used to feed ourselves and now have to depend on the Government for money. When I'm your Chief, I won't have fareWel anymore. Everyone will just get money. I'll give you money. With the chief in Las Vegas, we'll just take power. And when he gets back we'll kick him off the reserve. And we'll start gambling here. Wheels of fortune, and blackjack and slot machines. That's how we'll make our money. And we'll decide who's an Indian. No more of this blonde-haired, blue-eyed Bill C-31ers, coming on our reserve and taking our money. And the Indian religion. The true religion will be what we practise. No more of this whiteman's church. *(PHYLLIS shakes her head.)* And all Bazooka Joes will be in Saulteaux. *(TEDDY holds up a Bazooka Joe comic.)* All of you owe me something. Phyllis, you owe me money. Nigger, you owe me for taking out your tooth.)

NIGGER: Ka ween koosha ki kee wood tabi na seen ni wee wipid. Ka abi ni wee sa kaa dam. (You never took out the right one. And it's still hurting.)

TEDDY: Melvin ki masi na a mau ka kee weegi nan chi aihin truck, ta goo gravel chi aihin ki meeka nang. Shig oh ka keen Rachel ki masi na a mow chi pis nanabi ann, chi ki pa aman kidoon.

(Melvin, you owe me for helping you get gravel for your dad's road. And Rachel, you owe me to keep quiet, and keep my mouth shut.)

(RACHEL kicks over an empty chair.)

RACHEL: That's a lie.

MELVIN: What?

PHYLLIS: Rachel, don't.

TEDDY: Paa ka aka way hookerish. (Careful, you hooker slut.)

RACHEL: I don't owe you anything. He says you owe him for that gravel on your dad's road Melvin.

MELVIN: What?

TEDDY: I got you that gravel. You wouldn't even have got any if it wasn't for me. You're a Bill C-31er.

MELVIN: I got that gravel. You didn't...I even asked before you and yet they gave everyone gravel except for me. That's how you can tell who's Bill C-31 on this reserve. They're the ones with dirt on their roads.

TEDDY: That's 'cause you're not pure.

MELVIN: I'm more Indian than you. (TEDDY laughs.) In my heart. In my heart.

TEDDY: All you got is a card and some bullshit treaty number.

RACHEL: Teddy you're not even pure yourself. Your granny was part white.

TEDDY: Woo nab in, pisahnabin. (Sit down and shut up.)

RACHEL: Stop it Teddy. You don't even know what you're doing here. This is a joke. Look at this fuckin' sign with your stupid face on it. (RACHEL picks up one of the signs.) You're a joke. This whole thing is just more of the same.

TEDDY: Shut up.

RACHEL: NO. Can't you say anything more intelligent to me Teddy? Hunh? Maybe say, "Talk some more to me." Or I don't agree with you. Or anything. Anything that might tell me you're listening to me. To all of us. Instead of using us to help yourself.

TEDDY: You shut up. Or I'll tell everyone what you are.

RACHEL: What am I Teddy?

TEDDY: You know what this slut did?

RACHEL: You sleep with hookers.

TEDDY: How would you know that?

RACHEL: Because. You were gonna sleep with me.

PHYLLIS: What?

TEDDY: She's a whore. One time in Winnipeg, I phone the hooker escort service and tell them to send me over a real pretty one, and this is what they send me.

MELVIN: Is this true Rachel?

RACHEL: Does it matter if it is?

TEDDY: Of course it does. What kind of reserve would I be running here if I let hookers live here? Go on. Nobody wants you here. Mahjan. Akitten.

RACHEL: You're the only person I know who makes our language sound ugly. Why don't you go look after Margret and your baby, instead of making things worse for us.

TEDDY: (Grabs RACHEL by the hair.) You whore bitch.

RACHEL: Let me go.

TEDDY: You'd spread your legs for anyone with the money. I would never sleep with this disease. (He releases her.) She's not even proud of her own hair. Look at it. It's dyed. Indian hair. Black hair. She's embarrassed of it. It isn't even fuckin' clean.

NIGGER: That's enough.

TEDDY: Your damn rights it's enough.

            (TEDDY moves towards RACHEL who stops him with a pointed finger. She backs out the door.)

Get your black ass off my reserve.

            (MELVIN sits, lost.)

You too. Fuck off.

> (PHYLLIS grabs RACHEL's bag. As she does, TEDDY kicks her.)

NIGGER: Hey.

TEDDY: Shut up.

MELVIN: I have to go.

TEDDY: Sit down. Everyone shut the fuck up. Alright. Let's vote now. Who votes for Melvin? *(No one puts up their hand.)* Who votes for me? *(TEDDY puts up his hand and raises NIGGER's.)* Alright. Thank you. I accept your nomination as new chief. I will serve you good. Amen.

> *(End of ACT I.)*

ACT II

(The steps of the Partridge Pentecostal Church, the sign has been changed and it now reads "Creator's Church." "I Saw the Light" can be heard coming from within the church; it has a distinct country feel. The sound is slowly overpowered by a drum, beating slowly. The drum is accompanied by a song. "I Saw the Light" fades. MELVIN is sitting on the steps. He pulls a rag out of his pocket and twirls it around a bit. TEDDY enters.)

MELVIN: Boo-zhoo Teddy.

TEDDY: Boo-zhoo. What're you doing here Melvin?

MELVIN: Nothing.

TEDDY: Well go do nothing someplace else.

MELVIN: I don't want to go yet.

TEDDY: Take off.

MELVIN: You know why I come here?

TEDDY: To get in my way?

MELVIN: I come here so I won't sniff. This is the only place I can't sniff. I feel wrong about doing it here. I can't.

TEDDY: Then why do you still have that rag?

MELVIN: 'Cause when I leave here…I'll sniff again.

(MELVIN stands. TEDDY takes the rag out of MELVIN's hands. He almost has to wrestle him for it.)

TEDDY: Go on. Mahjan.

          (MELVIN leaves. TEDDY pulls out a cigarette and lights it. There is the sound of tires on gravel; headlights shine on TEDDY for a moment. A truck door opens and shuts. ROBERT enters. ROBERT sees that the church sign has changed and begins slowly climbing the steps.)

ROBERT: What is this?

TEDDY: (Church.)

ROBERT: This isn't a church. What have you done here?

TEDDY: The first part of self-government. Controlling our own spirits. No more white man's bullshit religion here. We go back to the ways we knew. That's the most important part of our people, our spirit.

ROBERT: And when you kill it we die.

TEDDY: I'm not killing anything.

ROBERT: What do you want?

TEDDY: I wanted to ask you something Robert.

ROBERT: Go ahead.

TEDDY: I was wondering if I could borrow five thousand bucks off you.

ROBERT: Why?

TEDDY: I want to make this one of the richest reserves in Manitoba.

ROBERT: I don't do that sort of thing.

TEDDY: Because it's me?

ROBERT: Because whenever I hear borrow it means give.

TEDDY: How 'bout this then, I give you back part of the church as collateral.

ROBERT: A church isn't a building Teddy.

TEDDY:	Do you see this? *(TEDDY points to the sign over the church.)* I did that. Nobody stopped me. And nobody will stop me when I get rid of every fuckin' Christian on this reserve.
ROBERT:	You can't.
TEDDY:	I keep hearing that. But you know what? I can.
ROBERT:	No one recognizes your authority.
TEDDY:	Then why is this place different now?
	(ROBERT is silent.)
	You know what I'm finding? It doesn't take much to make things different. Just a little effort. A little work. And money.
ROBERT:	I'm not giving you any.
TEDDY:	I'm not asking you to. I only want to "borrow" some. Not give. You and I want a lot of the same things. Every person on this reserve could be like you and Walter. But it won't happen unless a few of the smart guys like us go out and do it and give jobs to these people. We can give them jobs. Give them back some pride. We're both businessmen. I know you think you'll be just pissing your money away, so I'll offer you something. Now that I'm chief, I control housing. Houses need toilets. And septic tanks. And pipes. How many houses have you outfitted on this reserve in the last two years?
ROBERT:	I don't remember.
TEDDY:	That's 'cause there were none. Everybody knows the old chief and council hired a white guy in Ashern before they would hire you. You and I know they're jealous. But I'm not like that. I know that we need to work together. Like the church here. Maybe we could share it?
ROBERT:	No. I don't know.
TEDDY:	Think about it.
ROBERT:	Money isn't everything.

TEDDY: Sure it is. We want the same things for our people
            and our children. Simple things. Money. Jobs.
            Pride. Help me do it. Have you ever had real power
            Robert?

ROBERT: I've had money for a few years now.

TEDDY: Not that kind. Real power. Like what I have. It's
            good to be the chief. You can make things happen.
            We can make things happen.

ROBERT: I don't want that responsibility.

TEDDY: OK. Fine. Look, all I'm asking for is five thousand
            bucks. I guarantee you'll get it back.

ROBERT: How?

TEDDY: We're gonna be starting a casino here. With
            blackjack and slot machines and stuff. You'll get
            your money back in one week. One day.

ROBERT: I can't support that. Gambling's wrong.

TEDDY: Why?

ROBERT: It just is. It's not Christian.

TEDDY: Neither is having money. I thought rich people
            were supposed to give away all their money. Didn't
            Jesus say that?

ROBERT: That was just an example. I can help more people
            by having money than by having none.

TEDDY: Exactly. So can I. The casino's just the first part. I got
            plans to lease reserve land. And check if there's
            maybe gold or diamonds or stuff in the land. All
            kinds of things. But I need help. You're the only
            person I know who can help our people. That's why
            I'm asking for your help Robert.

ROBERT: You should have been a lawyer Teddy.

TEDDY: Why's that?

ROBERT: You can make bad ideas sound good.

TEDDY: How 'bout this, all I need from you is a maybe Robert. OK.? Just a maybe. Not a yes. But definitely not a no. Just a maybe. So I can start moving on this.

ROBERT: I'll have to think about it.

TEDDY: Good. Good. You do that. *(TEDDY shakes ROBERT's hand.)* You know one thing about trying to get money.

ROBERT: What's that?

TEDDY: It's easier pulling teeth.

(RACHEL and PHYLLIS are at PHYLLIS' house.)

PHYLLIS: You kids stop hitting that dog. Damn kids.

RACHEL: I need a cigrette.

PHYLLIS: There's still some butts left.

(RACHEL pockets the remaining butts.)

RACHEL: I'm gonna end up just like Nigger. I hate this place.

PHYLLIS: It prob'ly saved you.

(PHYLLIS moves to the kitchen and returns with some mouldy bread and two cans of sardines. She opens the fish and starts making sandwiches.)

RACHEL: What are you doing?

PHYLLIS: Making sandwiches for Schmidty's wake.

RACHEL: Those stink Phyllis. People aren't gonna eat those. Why don't you use salmon at least?

PHYLLIS: I used that last time.

RACHEL: Well use jam then.

PHYLLIS: None left. Sardines is all I got. My kids hate fish.

RACHEL: Aren't you s'posed to put them on toast?

PHYLLIS: My toaster's bust.

RACHEL: Use a hanger and the stove.

PHYLLIS: The hanger would melt.

RACHEL: You don't got metal ones?

PHYLLIS: Threw them out.

RACHEL: Why?

PHYLLIS: I like plastic ones better.

RACHEL: You shouldn't be making those for Schmidty's wake anyways. What are you gonna feed your kids?

PHYLLIS: I don't know yet.

RACHEL: Well you better start thinking about it.

PHYLLIS: Talk about something else alright?

RACHEL: No. No one around here wants to think about anything. They just want to keep pretending everything's alright, but it's not.

PHYLLIS: You be careful Rachel. You can hide in the roof here OK? That's where I used to hide so I didn't get beat up.

RACHEL: Forget it. I'm not hiding. And I'm not leaving. I'm not letting Teddy get away with this.

PHYLLIS: Quiet Rachel. OK? Please. Just let Teddy do self-government. Maybe he'll even get our welfare back for us.

RACHEL: Hey. He kicked you remember?

PHYLLIS: I know. But I've had lots worse things done to me than get kicked in the ass. You just have to be careful Rachel. Wait till the fareWel comes back and everything goes back to normal.

RACHEL: You call all this normal? You got no food to feed your kids. Or yourself. And what you do got you're giving away. Look at this bread. It's mouldy.

PHYLLIS: Oh. That's OK. They'll pray for it at church.

RACHEL: And what? It'll turn fresh.

PHYLLIS: No. People won't get sick then if they eat it.

RACHEL: Phyllis.

PHYLLIS: What?

RACHEL: Never mind.

PHYLLIS: Hey. You were wrong you know?

RACHEL: About what?

PHYLLIS: There was a Phyllis in the Bible. That big guy named Goliath. He was a Philis-tine.

RACHEL: That wasn't his name. That was his people.

PHYLLIS: I know. But there was still a Phyllis in the Bible.

RACHEL: Yeah and do you know what happened to that guy?

PHYLLIS: He got hit in the head with a rock.

RACHEL: Exactly.

PHYLLIS: So what. My name is still in the Bible.

RACHEL: OK Phyllis.

PHYLLIS: How come you didn't tell me Rachel?

RACHEL: Tell you what?

PHYLLIS: That you were a hooker.

RACHEL: Phyllis. I was a hooker.

PHYLLIS: Was it hard? That stuff you did. Being a hooker and that.

RACHEL: At first, but then I changed my name, and cut my hair.

PHYLLIS: So what was your name?

RACHEL: Simone. I wanted something French 'cause it sounds nice.

PHYLLIS: Simone? You should've picked Frenchy. Or else Buffy.

RACHEL: I was a hooker. Not a hairdresser.

PHYLLIS: So did it hurt?

RACHEL: Yeah. Sure it did.

PHYLLIS: Then how come you did that? Hookering.

RACHEL: When I was small I didn't even want to be anything. Nobody said to me you can be this or you can be that, and when I left here I saw what I was. For the first time.

PHYLLIS: What was that?

RACHEL: A woman. A Native woman. With no education. No money. No future.

PHYLLIS: I don't got those things neither Rachel yet I didn't become a hooker.

RACHEL: Maybe not, but I'll tell you something. To a lot of people you're worth about the same.

PHYLLIS: Even you?

RACHEL: No Phyllis. I didn't mean that. I'm just…shit.

PHYLLIS: What?

RACHEL: I don't even have time to feel bad about Schmidty being dead. I hate Teddy for doing all this.

PHYLLIS: How come he knew?

RACHEL: Like he said. He called the escort service. They sent me. I went to the hotel he was at. The Windsor. And when he opened the door. There I was.

PHYLLIS: Did he say anything?

RACHEL: Not at first. We just looked at each other. And then I tried to leave. But he wanted me to stay.

PHYLLIS: Did you?

RACHEL: No. I came home.

PHYLLIS: That's good.

(PHYLLIS gives pie plates to RACHEL.)

Here.

RACHEL: I'm not making pies.

(RACHEL gets up to leave.)

PHYLLIS: Where are you going?

RACHEL: I've got something to do.

PHYLLIS: What?

RACHEL: Women's work.

(Lights up on TEDDY's. There is an open pack of wieners and a bag of hotdog buns on the table. NIGGER puts a wiener in a bun, takes a bite, and then throws the bun away. They have a pile of papers in front of them. NIGGER and MELVIN are trying their best to "work". TEDDY's working hard, going through the papers. Smoking. The phone rings.)

TEDDY: Partridge Crop First Nation. Hunh? I don't know where the welfare money is. Yeah I'm the chief now. Yup. OK. *(He hangs up.)* What the hell was chief and council doing here? Look at this.

(NIGGER looks at the paper and nods his head as if he understands.)

What a mess.

NIGGER: Yeah eh.

MELVIN: It's people's own faults. They vote for them. They get what they deserve.

NIGGER: That's right. Me. I'm not voting for that chief and council again. I don't care how many two-fours they give me. How many did you get Melvin?

MELVIN: What's that?

NIGGER: Two-fours.

MELVIN: None. They just gave me gas slips.

TEDDY: Who'd you vote for anyways?

NIGGER: I forget.

(The phone rings.)

TEDDY: Partridge Crop First Nation. Yeah? Well how the hell am I supposed to know? I know I'm the chief. Call back later. *(TEDDY hangs up.)* Did you guys find those ledgers and shit yet?

MELVIN: Which ones?

TEDDY: The ones for health and education.

NIGGER: What do you need those for?

TEDDY: How the hell else you expect me to pay for the slot machines?

(The phone rings.)

Partridge Crop First Nation. What? You got a bobcat in your tree? Well what the hell am I supposed to do about it? Shoot it. *(TEDDY hangs up.)* People hear there's a new chief and all of a sudden I'm everybody's friend.

(The phone rings.)

Hello. How the hell am I supposed to know how to cook muskrat? *(TEDDY slams the phone down.)* Do either of you guys know how to type?

(NIGGER and MELVIN look at each other and shake their head.)

Well find those blank cheques— *(The phone rings. TEDDY practically rips the receiver off of the base.)* Quit phoning here. Oh. Sorry. I thought you were a band member. Forget it. Well get me the regional director of Indian Affairs then if I can't talk to the minister.

(TEDDY exits with the phone. NIGGER and MELVIN relax.)

NIGGER: What's this we're s'posed to be doing anyways?

MELVIN: Don't know.

NIGGER: There's gonna be one more good person on this reserve soon.

MELVIN: Who?

NIGGER: Me. Number three. That's gonna be me. It just about happened right now. Those dogs were chasing me and I fell on my head outside.

MELVIN: How come?

NIGGER: They were tryin' to bite me here. *(He points to his crotch.)* On the crutch.

MELVIN: Crotch. You gotta learn better English Nigger.

NIGGER: What for? I speak good English. I just sound funny 'cause of that time I burnt my tongue. I licked a hot pan. Someone cooked a cheese that time.

MELVIN: You're worse than an old dog you.

NIGGER: I was hungry. I bet I could've even ate a dog. Like Teddy's dog. That dog ate another dog that time at the church.

MELVIN: That was my dog that got ate.

NIGGER: I remember that little dog. He was all hairy. Boy that was a good dog. Too bad he got ate. I bet that hurt.

           (TEDDY returns.)

TEDDY: Well then if we're responsible give us full control. OK then if you want to be responsible start taking better care of us. I know. Fuck forget it alright, you call me back when you're ready to talk. What? Hey. I got two words for you buddy. Blockade. *(TEDDY slams the phone down and makes a sound of anger and frustration.)*

           (The phone rings.)

           I'm in a meeting.

(*NIGGER and MELVIN look at each other. NIGGER picks up the phone and gives the receiver to MELVIN, who gives it back to NIGGER, back and forth, until:*)

NIGGER: Ahneen Eh? Eh? Ehh? Yup. Ohhhh. Really? OK. OK. Eh? Yup. Tomorrow? Ehhunh. Bye.

(*NIGGER hangs up the phone.*)

TEDDY: Who was that?

NIGGER: Someone wants to clean our carpet for free.

(*TEDDY grabs the phone and redials.*)

TEDDY: Hey, where's my proposal for the gaming facility?

MELVIN: The what?

TEDDY: How 'bout those purchase orders?

NIGGER: What?

TEDDY: Jesus Christ, I've gotta do everything myself. One of you guys figure out how to work that fax machine. Hello? No don't...shit.

MELVIN: What?

TEDDY: I'm on hold.

(*TEDDY exits with the phone. NIGGER and MELVIN relax.*)

MELVIN: Hey Nigger. You got five bucks I can borrow?

NIGGER: I don't got no money. You only ask people who got money for money.

MELVIN: I already asked Robert.

NIGGER: That's 'cause you're s'posed to ask him for a job first. Then you get an advance from him. And then that's it.

MELVIN: Yeah?

NIGGER: Sure.

MELVIN:	I want my fareWel.
NIGGER:	Yeah. Me too.
MELVIN:	Are you gonna go to Schmidty's wake?
NIGGER:	Sure. How else am I gonna eat?
MELVIN:	Schmidty was a good man.
NIGGER:	Yeah. Even though he was drunk all the time.
MELVIN:	What am I?
NIGGER:	Eh?
MELVIN:	What kind of person am I?
NIGGER:	A man?
MELVIN:	No. What am I to you?
NIGGER:	Uhhh.
MELVIN:	Am I an Indian?
NIGGER:	Of course.
MELVIN:	Why?
NIGGER:	Why what?
MELVIN:	Why am I an Indian?
NIGGER:	'Cause you are.
MELVIN:	How do you know?
NIGGER:	Indians know other Indians. Even if they're part white. We're brothers and sisters. And we're warriors. All of us.
MELVIN:	I don't even speak Saulteaux.
NIGGER:	I'll teach you.
MELVIN:	I don't know why I want to be an Indian so bad. There's nothing good about being one.
NIGGER:	Sure there is. There's lots.

MELVIN: Like?

NIGGER: *(He thinks for a long while.)* You won't go bald-headed.

MELVIN: Hunh?

NIGGER: Indians don't get bald-headed. That's good. *(He thinks some more.)* And we're teachers. That's what Indians are. When white peoples came here a long time ago it was us who taught them. We showed them what to eat and we brought them turkey. And stuffing. And cranberries. That's what white people have Thanksgiving for. Except they don't share our turkey with us anymore.

MELVIN: Where'd you learn that?

NIGGER: In that book about Indians. That's where I know an Indian guy wrote *O Canada*. And you know what?

MELVIN: What?

NIGGER: We're gonna teach the white people again how to live.

MELVIN: How?

NIGGER: Lots more white people are gonna be poor. And they're gonna be on welfare. And because we already know how to live on welfare. We're gonna teach them how to live again.

            (TEDDY returns and hangs up. He lights another cigarette, mutters and goes through the papers. During the following, NIGGER starts whistling after constructing a "wiener flute".)

MELVIN: See Nigger. What is that?

NIGGER: What?

MELVIN: That thing in Teddy's hand.

NIGGER: A smoke.

MELVIN: Right? What do you do to a fish?

NIGGER: Eat it.

MELVIN: Or?

NIGGER: Catch it.

MELVIN: Or you can smoke it. Right?

NIGGER: Yeah.

MELVIN: OK. So you can smoke a fish. What's that coming out of that cigrette?

NIGGER: Smoke.

MELVIN: Right. Smoke coming out of a smoke. Or you can smoke a fish. Or smoke a cigrette or a cigrette's a smoke.

NIGGER: Oooooooohhhhhhh. I see. So. You can smoke a fish or a cigrette, or you can call a cigrette a smoke.

MELVIN: Yeah. It's just like "our home and native land." Native means two things.

NIGGER: Oooooooohhhhhhhh.

MELVIN: See. I can teach you English.

NIGGER: And I'll teach you Saulteaux.

MELVIN: I smell tacos.

TEDDY: Will you guys shut up?

NIGGER: He's just telling me about smoke.

TEDDY: Fuck that. Listen. We got to get moving on this casino. Blackjack and dice and stuff. And slot machines. That's my big plan. Once that's under way we'll be more than self-sufficient.

MELVIN: But gambling isn't a good thing. We'd be playing our own casino.

TEDDY: Only white people would be allowed to play. No Indians. Besides, now that we're self-governing who gives a shit where the money comes from.

(*Noticing NIGGER's whistling.*) What the fuck are you doing?

NIGGER: (*Eats the wiener.*) Since I don't got no fiddle I make a wiener flute. I was almost Manitoba whistle champ too eh. In 1968. But I got beat up and I had a fat lip. So I couldn't whistle good that day. That guy who beat me up knocked out a tooth too.

(*MELVIN sniffs NIGGER's head.*)

MELVIN: That's you. Your head smells like tacos.

NIGGER: It's this stupid sock. It's supposed to make my tooth better.

MELVIN: You should buy a new one. It stinks.

NIGGER: I was gonna. But I didn't get my cheque.

MELVIN: So is this the new band office?

TEDDY: Assholes. I'm surrounded by assholes.

(*NIGGER starts looking in the ashtray for a good butt. TEDDY punches his hand.*)

Fuck sakes. Stop screwing around. We have business here. We have to take care of things. We're men. Right? Right?

(*MELVIN and NIGGER look at each other.*)

We'll also have to keep an eye on those stupid women.

MELVIN: What stupid women?

TEDDY: That hooker and her fat friend.

MELVIN: Rachel's not a hooker anymore.

TEDDY: We can't have hookers on this reserve. It's not good for our kids seeing that.

MELVIN: What about guys who sleep with hookers?

TEDDY: Shut up you halfbreed.

MELVIN: You too. Your granny was white.

NIGGER: Yeah Teddy. You too.

TEDDY: Both of you shut up. You're lucky I even let you stay here. I can get rid of all you Bill-C31ers. You're just a bunch of mooches. Taking away from us real Indians. Nigger. I've got a job for you.

NIGGER: Yeah?

TEDDY: Yeah. I'm giving you Schmidty's job.

MELVIN: What?

NIGGER: Really?

MELVIN: He can't even read but.

TEDDY: Pisahnabin. I'm chief. I pick who I want. Besides. I can't hire you Melvin. You're Bill C-31. No 31ers can work for the Partridge Crop First Nation.

NIGGER: Thank you Teddy.

TEDDY: You're welcome.

MELVIN: This is bullshit. I'm an Indian too. I can work.

TEDDY: Yeah?

MELVIN: Yeah.

TEDDY: OK then. I'm gonna need someone to pick up my slot machines. The only thing is, I don't have a truck. You know anyone with a truck Melvin?

MELVIN: Cheezie's got one.

TEDDY: That's not a truck, that's a piece of shit. Those slot machines are heavy man. We need a good, solid vehicle.

MELVIN: Robert's got one.

TEDDY: That's right eh?

MELVIN: Yeah. Brand new too.

TEDDY: Really?

MELVIN: But he'd never lend us. He doesn't do that sort of thing.

TEDDY: I know. That's too bad we can't get that vehicle. Our casino's gonna need a manager. Someone who's good with numbers.

MELVIN: I'm good with numbers.

NIGGER: That's right. He taught me math. Eh Melvin?

MELVIN: I can run a casino.

TEDDY: I believe you Melvin. I believe you. But we kinda… need that truck.

MELVIN: I can ask Robert, but I don't think he'll—

TEDDY: How 'bout if you just "borrow" it for a while.

MELVIN: You mean steal it?

TEDDY: Borrow. Didn't you used to borrow cars before in Winnipeg?

MELVIN: Yeah. But I couldn't do that to Robert.

TEDDY: Tell you what Melvin. Not only will I make you casino manager. I'll make you an Indian.

MELVIN: Government already did that.

TEDDY: That doesn't mean anything. I can make you a real Indian.

MELVIN: How?

TEDDY: It's spiritual. And hey, if you don't want to do it, you won't have a job. And I'll always remember you chickening out. Indians don't chicken out from nothing.

          (MELVIN thinks for a while.)

MELVIN: OK. Aow i tha Nigger.

NIGGER: That's good Saulteaux. See. I told you you were an Indian.

(MELVIN leaves.)

TEDDY: I need you to be responsible for distributing the money for what I call Treaty Day every day.

NIGGER: What?

TEDDY: Yes. Since there's no more fareWel, I'm taking this initiative to keep people from starving. So all the adults will get five dollars a day every day.

NIGGER: Really? From you?

TEDDY: No. From the government, and then from the casino.

NIGGER: So I'd be the new Treaty Day every day money guy?

TEDDY: Yes.

NIGGER: What about the kids?

TEDDY: We need to have priorities. Besides, it's only temporary, until everyone on the reserve has a job.

NIGGER: Hey, can I get my cheque?

TEDDY: For what?

NIGGER: For my new job.

TEDDY: You haven't even worked yet.

NIGGER: I just want an advance.

TEDDY: Forget it.

NIGGER: How 'bout my fareWel cheque then?

TEDDY: No more fuckin' fareWel. I told you, from now on it's gonna be Treaty Day every day.

NIGGER: When?

TEDDY: Soon. As soon as I secure some interim funding.

NIGGER: OK. Gimme my Treaty money then.

(TEDDY sighs. He takes out his wallet and throws five dollars at NIGGER.)

TEDDY: Here. Stick it up your ass.

NIGGER: Thank you chief. See that.

TEDDY: What?

NIGGER: That works for getting money too.

TEDDY: What's that?

NIGGER: Bugging the shit out of someone till they give it to you. You can do that too when you go to Ottawa. Just bug the shit out of them.

TEDDY: Sometimes Nigger...you're smart. *(TEDDY snatches the five dollars out of NIGGER's hand.)*

NIGGER: Hey. That's mine.

TEDDY: I know. But you owe me ten bucks remember?

NIGGER: Oh. Can I get my fiddle back then?

TEDDY: Yes. For fuck sakes. YES. Take it.

(TEDDY storms out. NIGGER takes his fiddle.)

(Lights up on RACHEL, waiting for NIGGER. Steps of the church. Whistling can be heard. NIGGER enters, carrying his fiddle.)

NIGGER: Ahneen.

RACHEL: Cahngoot.

NIGGER: You better watch out. Those dogs'll come after you.

RACHEL: I'm not afraid of them.

NIGGER: You're not afraid of lots I think.

RACHEL: Just the future.

NIGGER: Yeahup. That's why we have to be strong today. *(Showing off his fiddle.)* It's nice eh?

RACHEL: Yeah.

NIGGER: Boy, I missed my fiddle. I didn't have it for so long

I was just about gonna take up piano, but you can't carry those. I'm never gonna pawn my fiddle again. Unless I need money. What are you doing here anyways?

RACHEL: I need your help.

NIGGER: Really?

RACHEL: Yeah.

NIGGER: OK.

RACHEL: I need you to bless this for me. *(She gives him the outfit.)*

NIGGER: Boy. It's been a long time since I saw this. This is Angus's?

(RACHEL nods.)

How'd you get it?

RACHEL: Phyllis gave me.

NIGGER: Boy, this is very old.

RACHEL: Is it OK for me to use?

NIGGER: You should ask Walter.

RACHEL: I can't find him.

NIGGER: How come you're asking me?

RACHEL: Because. You're an Elder.

NIGGER: No one's said that to me before. That I'm an Elder.

RACHEL: Can I use this?

NIGGER: What does your heart tell you?

RACHEL: Yes.

NIGGER: OK then.

RACHEL: I only got two butts. I don't have no other tobacco to give you.

NIGGER: That's OK. You gave me tobacco before. I remember. How come you need this?

RACHEL: I need to make someone listen. To see who I am. To respect me.

NIGGER: OK then. Wait here. I'll be right back.

RACHEL: Thank you for blessing this Sheldon.

NIGGER: Ahh that's OK. Thank you for the butts.

(Lights up on Walter's. PHYLLIS is by the counter. She plops a little pail of saskatoons on the counter.)

PHYLLIS: Walterrr. I brought you some saskatooooons that my kids picked. And a saandwiich. I want to buy some stuff in your store with my cheque. OK? Walter?

(PHYLLIS sits. ROBERT enters.)

ROBERT: Have you seen my truck?

PHYLLIS: No.

ROBERT: Somebody stole my truck.

PHYLLIS: What? When?

ROBERT: I don't know. And people wonder why I never lend them anything? I guess I don't have to if they're just gonna take it anyways.

PHYLLIS: Maybe you forgot it somewhere.

ROBERT: It's a truck. Not a set of keys.

PHYLLIS: Well don't get mad at me. I didn't take your stupid truck.

ROBERT: Teddy's behind this. I should've put a stop to all this nonsense a long time ago.

PHYLLIS: You mean self-government?

ROBERT: A farce is more like it. Have you seen Melvin?

PHYLLIS: I bet that's who's got your truck. Melvin used to steal cars all the time. He even tried to steal mine, but it wouldn't start.

ROBERT: That's it. I'm calling the police.

PHYLLIS: Relax. I was just kidding.

ROBERT: You can tell me to relax when someone steals your property.

PHYLLIS: I don't have any property.

ROBERT: And that's why you're stuck here.

PHYLLIS: What's the matter with you?

ROBERT: I'm sick of this place. I'm sick of no one respecting me. I'm the only one around here besides Walter who owns a business. I'm the only one around here who works. I'm the only one around here who cares about this community. But not no more. That's it. I've had enough.

(MELVIN walks in. Spooked.)

Where's my truck Melvin?

(MELVIN motions with his lips towards outside. ROBERT walks out. MELVIN sits.)

PHYLLIS: What's the matter with you? Melvin what's wrong?

(ROBERT comes back.)

ROBERT: You fuckin' asshole. It wasn't enough you had to steal my brand new truck but you go and wreck it too.

(ROBERT grabs MELVIN. PHYLLIS stops him.)

What's with you fuckin' Indians hunh? Get a job. Get off welfare. Stop taking my things.

PHYLLIS: Wait. Robert. Wait. Melvin, what's wrong?

ROBERT: The mirror's all smashed.

PHYLLIS: Robert shut up. Someone's dead. Who Melvin? Who's dead? Rachel? Is it Rachel?

MELVIN: Nigger.

PHYLLIS: What?

MELVIN: He's dead.

ROBERT: When?

PHYLLIS: Where Melvin?

MELVIN: On the road. Just a little while ago.

PHYLLIS: What happened?

MELVIN: I hit him.

ROBERT: With my truck? *(ROBERT sits and hangs his head.)*

PHYLLIS: Where is he?

MELVIN: In the ditch.

ROBERT: You just left him there?

MELVIN: He's dead. I killed him.

PHYLLIS: Number three.

MELVIN: It was an accident. He jumped at me. It was an accident. It's all Teddy's fault. He made me steal your truck Robert. He told me I'd be an Indian if I helped him get his slot machines.

ROBERT: Slot machines?

             (TEDDY walks in.)

PHYLLIS: Teddy. Nigger is dead.

TEDDY: What?

PHYLLIS: Melvin killed him.

MELVIN: It was an accident.

TEDDY: What? What the hell are you talking about?

PHYLLIS: He was prob'ly sniffing.

MELVIN: No.

ROBERT:	Of course. A sniffer and a thief.
TEDDY:	Someone talk to me.
PHYLLIS:	Nigger. He's dead.
ROBERT:	Because of you Teddy.
TEDDY:	I wasn't driving your stupid truck.
MELVIN:	You made me steal it. You made me.
ROBERT:	If you wanted my truck why didn't you just ask me?
TEDDY:	Eh? You've never done anything to help anyone on this reserve. Ever. Don't try act all good now.
PHYLLIS:	Poor Nigger. Poor Nigger.
MELVIN:	I didn't mean...
ROBERT:	If you hadn't played your stupid politics none of this would've happened. Self-government. You've gotten someone killed now.
TEDDY:	I'm not responsible for that.
ROBERT:	Of course you are. This is why self-government will never work. Because there'll always be people like you.
TEDDY:	And people like you too Robert. Telling us to stay the same.
ROBERT:	So irresponsible.
TEDDY:	So chicken-shit.
ROBERT:	Selfish.
TEDDY:	I'm selfish.
ROBERT:	Fuckin' heathen.
TEDDY:	Goddamned Christian.

(ROBERT takes a swing at TEDDY. PHYLLIS jumps in between them.)

PHYLLIS: Hey. Hey…

                *(All, save MELVIN who is sitting, start yelling at
                one another. Chaos. RACHEL enters wearing the
                outfit, her breasts bared. PHYLLIS, TEDDY and
                ROBERT fall silent. They all stare at RACHEL,
                who begins to dance slowly. The sound of a drum
                and a song builds as she dances. She stops. RACHEL
                and TEDDY move towards each other. There is no
                sound. NIGGER hobbles in. He's missing a shoe. He
                picks up a Pepsi, bag of chips, bar and a handful of
                Bazooka Joes. He notices the saskatoons and drops all
                the junk food and starts eating the saskatoons. His
                other eye is now also black and the sock is no longer
                tied around his head. PHYLLIS screams and hides
                behind ROBERT. Everyone stares at NIGGER in
                fear and awe.)*

NIGGER: Boy Walter, you got any Bazooka Joe with
                Saulteaux on them? What? What the hell's the
                matter with you guys?

MELVIN: You're dead. I hit you. I saw you. Lying in the ditch.

PHYLLIS: You're dead. You're dead.

NIGGER: Yeah? *(He notices RACHEL and smiles.)* Now I
                remember Rachel.

TEDDY: What the hell happened to you?

NIGGER: I got hit. Just like a dog. Whooom. *(NIGGER makes a
                motion with his hand.)* Katuck. I woke up in the ditch.

MELVIN: You jumped at me.

                (Everyone looks at NIGGER.)

NIGGER: I didn't. I was walking on the road and I slipped. I
                slipped on dog shit. You know, that's just like my
                life. Always almost. I was almost a good man. This
                is what people on this reserve thought of me. I was
                almost a good man. That time I got sick. That time I
                got 'monia in my heart, and I almost died. People
                said I was a good man. Not the time I was Manitoba
                fiddle champ in 1972. Or that time that cop car hit

me and I shared my ten thousand bucks with everybody. Or that time I brought this reserve its first TV for *Hockey Night in Canada*. They never said I was a good man those times. I was almost, but I wasn't. 'Cause I didn't die. I got better. And this time, you know what?

RACHEL: What?

NIGGER: I did die. I saw this...never mind. It wasn't all that great anyways. I was almost a good man. I just wish I could be that. A good man. Hey the Chief's back from Vegas.

TEDDY: When?

NIGGER: Just a little while ago. Jim Sinclair saw him driving a brand new Cadillac. You know what but?

MELVIN: What?

NIGGER: That truck fixed my sore tooth.

            (NIGGER holds up his tooth.)

ROBERT: Did the welfare cheques arrive?

NIGGER: Don't know. I was lying in the ditch.

MELVIN: Let's go find your shoe. Can you give us a lift Robert?

            (ROBERT looks at MELVIN and leaves. NIGGER and MELVIN look at each other and exit.)

TEDDY: Where you guys going? Come back here. You guys...

PHYLLIS: I'm gonna get my cheque. You coming Rachel?

            (RACHEL shakes her head.)

            I gotta go. I'll see you at Schmidty's wake Rachel.

            (PHYLLIS exits.)

TEDDY: It was different here. I made it different. What do you want Rachel?

RACHEL:	What do you see Teddy?
TEDDY:	Whore.
RACHEL:	Yeah Teddy. I was a whore. I've been fucked many times. It's made me strong.
TEDDY:	I didn't want to hurt you Rachel.
RACHEL:	You can't hurt me. You never could. What do you see Teddy?
TEDDY:	Ikwe. A Native woman.
RACHEL:	And I see. A man. A Native man. A strong man, but one who's afraid. Afraid because I know you. I know you men, and what you want. When you'd go in me, I could feel your heart. Beating. And when you were finished, laying on top of me I could still feel your life beating faster. What you were. What you are. What you could be. But it's time to make things right. To say goodbye to the things that keep us down. Our people's future comes from the past. Not male or female. Pure or mixed. Christian or Traditional. It's all these things. Together. Respected.
	(Lights up on the window. MELVIN, NIGGER and PHYLLIS are there.)
PHYLLIS:	Did that truck hurt Nigger?
NIGGER:	Nahh. That time I got rolled and thrown in a dumpster and then I got crushed in the back of a garbage truck hurt worse.
PHYLLIS:	They always make us wait eh?
NIGGER:	Yeah.
PHYLLIS:	They better be here. Or else I'm gonna get my kids and then we're gonna camp out here.
NIGGER:	Camping don't get you money. You need relatives. Me. I'm gonna burn down the band office if they don't give us our cheques.
PHYLLIS:	Come on.

NIGGER: If I had a crutch these guys would be in big trouble.

(MELVIN starts kicking and hitting the window.)

MELVIN: Not this again. You fuckers. Where the hell's our money? You're making us starve and live in shit. I'm sick of it. You hear that? Are you hearing me? I'll kill you. I'll kill all of you. You fuckers. I hate this. Do you hear me?

(MELVIN pulls out his Treaty card and rips it in half.)

PHYLLIS: Don't Melvin.

(PHYLLIS gives MELVIN back the two halves of his card. The window slides open. Three cheques fall out. NIGGER and PHYLLIS pick up their cheques quickly.)

NIGGER: Boy that's a new way of getting money I never seen before.

PHYLLIS: See. I told you they'd come.

NIGGER: It's about time. Where the hell were these anyways?

PHYLLIS: Prob'ly in Vegas. I heard the chief won lots of money in Vegas. And even a Cadillac. Maybe that's how come we're getting cheques, he won our money back.

(PHYLLIS picks up MELVIN's cheque.)

PHYLLIS: Here Melvin. This one's yours.

(A long pause before MELVIN finally takes the cheque.)

MELVIN: Bunch of fuckers.

NIGGER: What you gonna buy with your cheque?

PHYLLIS: I don't know. Food. I guess.

NIGGER: Me. I'm gonna buy toothpaste. What about you Melvin?

MELVIN: Hunh?

NIGGER: What are you gonna buy with your cheque?

MELVIN: I don't know. You know what?

PHYLLIS: What?

MELVIN: That felt really good just now.

NIGGER: What?

MELVIN: Getting mad. It made me feel like...an Indian.

             *(The scene opens on the steps of the Partridge Crop
             Pentecostal Church of the Creator. A song can be
             heard from inside the church. Its melody is "Jesus in
             the Family", but the word "Jesus" isn't said. The
             rhythm is a cross between the country feel of earlier
             and the drum. RACHEL is sitting on the steps.
             NIGGER exits the church, eating a sandwich. He
             has a woman's shoe on one foot. The sound of
             children and a dog playing can be heard.)*

NIGGER: Boy Rachel, what're you doing?

RACHEL: Nothing.

NIGGER: Oh *(NIGGER sits beside her.)* I'm sad Schmidty died.

RACHEL: Me too.

NIGGER: You been in there yet?

             (RACHEL shakes her head.)

             I've never seen nothing like that before. Half this
             place Christians. Half Traditional. And nobody
             fighting. That's good eh?

RACHEL: Yeah.

NIGGER: You want some of this samich? It kind of stinks, but
             it's pretty good. I think it's little fish. Since my tooth
             got fixed I eat fish again.

RACHEL: No thanks.

NIGGER: You think these little fish come from B.C.?

RACHEL: Prob'ly.

NIGGER: I'm gonna go to B.C. Get some little fish samich.

RACHEL: Hm.

NIGGER: What the hell's the matter with you anyways?

RACHEL: Do you got a cigrette?

NIGGER: *(Pats himself down for a butt and then takes off his shoe and gives her some matches.)* Nope. I got a match. Look. *(NIGGER lifts up his pant leg to show off a brand new white sock.)* I got a new sock with my cheque.

RACHEL: Where's the other one?

NIGGER: What other one?

RACHEL: Forget it.

NIGGER: *(He pulls up his other pant leg to show his old grey sock.)* This sock still smells like tacos. Too bad it don't taste like tacos. You think they got tacos in B.C.?

RACHEL: Mexico maybe.

NIGGER: Yeah eh?

RACHEL: How come you got a woman's shoe on?

NIGGER: Me and Melvin couldn't find my other one, so we went to the dump. I liked this one. Did you get your fareWel cheque yet?

RACHEL: No.

> *(The sound of a truck pulling up, a door opening and closing. ROBERT enters.)*

NIGGER: Ahneen boy. You want some fish samich?

ROBERT: No.

NIGGER: I didn't mean to hit your truck. I'm sorry 'bout that Robert.

ROBERT: What'd you do to my dog Nigger?

NIGGER: Nothing.

ROBERT: What's with this place hunh? First you people steal
               my truck. Then someone goes and knocks my dog's
               teeth out.

RACHEL: What?

ROBERT: Why would someone do that? It's sick. Why?

NIGGER: Maybe he was biting people.

RACHEL: Stop complaining Robert.

ROBERT: No. That was my best dog. Do you know I kept him
               the longest without anything happening to him?
               And that was two years. They shoot my dogs. They
               try to burn my steps. They're fuckin' concrete. They
               don't burn. But does that stop them? If they had any
               balls they'd burn my house, but then I guess I'd just
               get a bigger one and then they'd burn that. Why'd
               they have to do that to my dog?

RACHEL: I don't know.

NIGGER: Maybe they thought he had a toothache.

ROBERT: Shut up Nigger.

RACHEL: Where are you going?

ROBERT: I'm getting out. I'm taking my family to Winnipeg.
               Taking them away from all this. There's no future
               here.

               (ROBERT leaves.)

NIGGER: You should go with him.

RACHEL: No. I hate this place. But it's my home.

NIGGER: That Schmidty's lucky being dead. Everyone gets
               to be a good man but me. How come people aren't
               afraid to talk bad about you while you're alive, but
               not good? They only talk good about you when
               you're dead. I shoulda stayed dead.

RACHEL: You're a good man Sheldon.

NIGGER: Yeah?

RACHEL: Yeah.

NIGGER: How come?

RACHEL: 'Cause you don't die.

> *(TEDDY and MELVIN enter.)*

MELVIN: We gotta go right to Ottawa. Tell them we're not gonna take it anymore.

TEDDY: Yeah. Yeah.

RACHEL: Hey you guys. You know what?

MELVIN: What?

RACHEL: Sheldon's a good man.

MELVIN: So I knew that.

TEDDY: Hey Nigger. I took care of that dog for you.

NIGGER: Which one?

TEDDY: The one that bit you.

NIGGER: Yeah? Meegwetch.

MELVIN: And you know what else Teddy?

TEDDY: What?

MELVIN: I'm an Indian. I'm an Indian.

TEDDY: I know.

> *(TEDDY looks at RACHEL, smiles and then goes into the church.)*

MELVIN: I'm going to Ottawa.

RACHEL: When?

MELVIN: I don't know. Later.

NIGGER: Boy I'll go with you. You can get mad and I'll just bug the shit out of them.

RACHEL: Do you got a cigrette Melvin?

MELVIN: No. *(MELVIN twirls his rag.)* Quitting this is like being a Christian to me. It's hard. Hey you know what but?

(RACHEL shakes her head. MELVIN takes out the two halves of his Treaty card.)

I figured out I'm an Indian from these two parts of my Treaty card. See. My face is on one half and my number is on the other half. That picture is what people see. The number is what the government sees. And the card's like me. In two parts. Part white. Part Indian. And you put them together. And you get an Indian. Me. But not 'cause the government says so. 'Cause I said so. I had to get mad to find that out. That's good eh?

RACHEL: Yes.

MELVIN: And you know what else?

RACHEL: Hmm?

(MELVIN removes a five dollar bill.)

MELVIN: I found five bucks on the road. *(He looks up at the sign.)* They keep changing this place's name. They should just call it Ahnamay igamik..

(RACHEL looks at MELVIN.)

RACHEL: That's good Melvin. You said that good.

MELVIN: Thanks. Nigger taught me.

(NIGGER is embarrassed. PHYLLIS runs in, out of breath.)

PHYLLIS: Rachel. Rachel, guess what?

RACHEL: What?

PHYLLIS: I got money. Look. *(PHYLLIS shows RACHEL some money.)* I got my cheque cashed.

MELVIN: I didn't cash mine yet. The chief said, "It won't never happen again." But he's still gonna go to Vegas.

PHYLLIS: I didn't cash my fareWel cheque. I meant my other cheque. From the Partridge Crop Band Office.

RACHEL: That cheque was no good.

PHYLLIS: No. Walter cashed it for me. He said OK. He said he liked the saskatoons and to thank my kids for picking them.

NIGGER: What saskatoons?

PHYLLIS: The ones in the bush. My kids were getting hungry so they started eating them. Then I remembered Walter liked those eh, so I made my kids pick some and I gave him. And he cashed my cheque. Here. Melvin. I got five bucks now.

MELVIN: That's OK. I found some already.

(The sound of the children and the dog increases.)

Hey you kids. Come here.

PHYLLIS: They don't even play at the dump anymore.

MELVIN: That's 'cause nobody's got good garbage anymore. Hey you kids. Come here. I'll teach you how to be an Indian.

(MELVIN leaves to join them. NIGGER follows.)

NIGGER: Boy, Melvin. You got five bucks I could borrow?

(PHYLLIS sits beside RACHEL.)

PHYLLIS: What's wrong?

RACHEL: I love this place.

PHYLLIS: I know. But it's our home. You know what's funny?

RACHEL: Hmm?

PHYLLIS: When the fareWel disappeared I got scared and then I wanted it back really bad. And now that it's back I kind of don't want it anymore. That's weird eh?

RACHEL: No. It's not weird. You always think goodbyes are
              bad. But sometimes they're good. D'you have any
              smokes?

                      (PHYLLIS reaches into her jacket and pulls out a
                      fresh pack of smokes. She opens them and offers one
                      to RACHEL. RACHEL takes it. PHYLLIS also
                      takes a smoke. RACHEL lights her cigarette and
                      then PHYLLIS's.)

              That's good.

                      (They smoke. Lights out.)

              The End